GETTING HERE

— poems —

[2020 HINDSIGHT]

*

Tomasz Dubito

Chapbook Press

Schuler Books
2660 28th Street SE
Grand Rapids, MI 49512
(616) 942-7330
www.schulerbooks.com

Getting Here - Poems

ISBN 13: 9781966196501

eBook ISBN: 9781966196518

Library of Congress Control Number: 2025923759

Printed in the United States by Chapbook Press.

If you would be a poet, *"write living newspapers … be a reporter from outer space, filing dispatches to some supreme managing editor who believes in full disclosure and has a low tolerance for bullshit."*

– *Lawrence Ferlinghetti* - "Poetry as Insurgent Art"

And you may ask yourself

"Well … How did I get here?"

Talking Heads – "Once In A Lifetime"

No matter where you go, there you are.

- *Earl Mac Rauch* -

"The Adventures of Buckaroo Banzai Across the Eighth Dimension"

* * *

The goings-on and subject matter put forward in this collection have their origin in the journals Mr Dubito kept throughout a decade of therapy where he was routinely presented with what he said felt like a tossed salad of platitudes about how best to deal with day-to-day episodic periods of anxiety, fear, anger, migraines, depression, paralyzing indecision, nightmares … and deteriorating relationships.

*

To be fair, having received a VA assessment for combat-related PTSD, navigating the sensory gumbo that is life – with a 70% mental disability as his guide – was not part of any reality anyone could have realistically prepared him for.

He journaled to orient himself, seeking to better understand how memory and emotion interact. With a stretch goal of expanding his comfort zone beyond the implicit borders of survival mode, he wrote. A lot.

As his efforts with observational writing improved he began building stories – which led to experimenting with 'found' poetry; then concrete poems, poems of witness, prose, free verse, sonnets, lists, satire, and absurdities – which prompted this book.

*

You may find that one or more of his poems offer a different form or perspective from what you may be accustomed to. Mr Dubito sez it's because he's seein' the world a bit differently now that he's begun confronting his ghosts and demons. While he informs us there were some difficult things needed sayin', like – *I have a mental disability*, casting a weary eye toward the general population he's thinking – *maybe we all do*.

*

Because of 2020's gradual accumulation of layers, Mr Dubito chose not to paginate this fragmented reconstruction. To smartly explore his unnumbered mosaic, Mr Dubito recommends liberal use of indie bookmarks, and occasional random contemplations.

– unattributed – July 4th ~ Independence Day: 2025

(And yeah, well, Democracy was fun while it lasted)

SEARCHING FOR THE VOICE THAT IS

great
within us
Mr Dubito finds
ruinous fragments
of masculine objects
lead-heavy wickedness
righteous indignation
politics of racism
bigotry, abuse
and the dark
laughter
of law

Mr Dubito
daydreams like a
pensive sniper, but
he also fancies he's like
Szymborska, trapped in
beguiling fictions amid
the leaky boundaries
of death and pain

CONTENTS ~   PREFACE

(7) [2020 HINDSIGHT — July — ROCKIN' & ROLLIN']

      CLEMENCY

      MOTHERS

      THE NEIGHBOR'S WIFE

      MY LEARNING PLATFORM

      OF COURSE

      NEIGHBORS: July ...

(8) [2020 HINDSIGHT — August — TOTAL RECALL]

      TIMING THE THUNDER

      FAMILY MATTERS

      KODAK MOMENTS

      TWENTY QUESTIONS

      MOM MODE

      CREMAINS

      MR DUBITO WRITES A DEATH POEM

      OBSERVATIONS

(9) [2020 HINDSIGHT — September — WAS LIKE BEES IN MY HEAD]

      BULLETPROOF: bag o' tricks

      A LACK OF SIMILARITY TO SOMETHING ELSE

      UNREPENTANT

      EDICT OF GRACE

      AFTER THE VIVISEPULTURE

      THE KULESHOV EFFECT

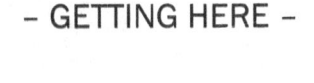

– GETTING HERE –

(1) — SOMETHING WAS LIKELY TO HAPPEN

President Trump said that he'd been briefed on the outbreak of a new virus from China and that the United States had the situation *"toad-a-lee under control"* and that he was *"not-at-all"* concerned about the possibility of a pandemic. *"It's going to be fine."*

But, it wasn't, was it

cuz as you & I both now know

just because he thought and talked shit

didn't mean that made it so . . .

Climbing the stairs that day, you became keenly aware

of the tension between freedom and restriction, as if

fleetingly glimpsed behind a door — or appearing

in a rainy window — a cognitive distortion that

was both hesitant and blurred, like in 1903

when Topsy, the Coney Island elephant

killed her third handler in 3 years

and in a display to discredit

a new technology, was

Westinghoused

by Thomas

Edison

MAYBE I NEED TO TALK ABOUT THIS

1.

Driving down a country road, my mind's eye

meanders into my adolescence and I remember

how "talkin' back" to my parents was *sassin'*

and did not go unpunished:

>*Do you want me to hit you!?!*

>*You just wait 'til your father gets home!!*

"Bein' schooled" also meant – relentless

bullying by a bat-shit crazy boy –

>*You want me to hit you again, don't you?*

Identity development & nurturing

were like psychotically conjoined

home and away games

2.

(*Branta canadensis*) I remember thinking as the honking

Canada goose hurled itself at my car like a metaphor in

a Greek myth. The road was not narrow where I left it

twerking rural traffic to a standstill; the widening silence

of an aluminum night took possession of my misadventure

3.

During a session with my therapist, she tells me

Active Shooter Drills are now a new normal for schools ...

       later, listening to Lead Belly's harmonies

capture continuous joy and pain, I am still shaking

my head at this, childhood memories, and

whatever the hell that goose was thinking.

Life is like that, you know, how it

     hits you, *again* and *again*

       with *shit* that makes no sense.

Unresolved issues somehow becoming tied to

Active Shooter Drills, amid concerns that

the orbit of your body is disengaged

from the direction of its spin

      like Mercury ...

       in retrograde.

ON THE IMPACT OF WAR TRAUMA ... during a New Year's Eve celebration

Fear, dread ... an uneasiness

causes you to sweat

feel restless   TENSE [!]   have

a Rapid Heartbeat ... you may

even feel abandoned.

Faced with what   to you

sounds like heavy weapons

you become like a variation

in a thought experiment

about Schrödinger's cat –

neither alive nor dead.

DISEMBODIED

Conversational A.I. and chatbots can now automate customer resolutions with intelligent virtual agent technology and serve more customers at a lower cost

you had no other

choice but to play by the rules

of a decision tree, followed by music

-on-hold that sounds vaguely like Kenny-G's

'Songbird' – mixed with vain repetitions of prayer

"Hello - CHATBOT will see you now."

CHATBOT: *Are you distressed, shocked, excited, or in paaaain?*

Press 1 for yes, 2 for no.   [1]

CHATBOT: *Are you currently experiencing ecological disruption iiin-a metropolis, forest, or jungle?*

Press 1 for yes, 2 for no.   [2]

CHATBOT: *Do you currently have access to nuclear weapons, fossil fuels, clear drinking water, first aaaaid supplies?   Thank you for your call.*

***

(DISEMBODIED VOICE IN HALLWAY)

– *You're sighing*

Did you take your pill? –

REDEMPTION

Fort Carson
WARRIOR TRANSITION UNIT:

These are oddly fragile moments:

> Shards lay strewn in whitewashed allusions
> Spring-loaded phrases snap at their victims
> Even the quiet is harsh   Searching for Alice
> in a palace, you think of a ONCE UPON A TIME story –

> how the Tigris was once moonstruck – and how
> you trembled in your trance having seen her double
> -veiled dance arouse a seraphic Euphrates in
> the ancient Cradle of Civilization ...

[Several men are now running toward him]

> This is before the incident in Mosul/
> Before the recurring nightmares/B4
> the alarm & burn of clear flame and
> the arrival of a tireless interpreter:

> *Do you comprehend what I have said*
> *Tell them what they want to know*
> *or they will make you*
> *wish that you were dead*

[Charcoal is the first ingredient]

In a ghoulish desert dream: a pillowcase
stripped from its pillow/removed from the bed
stuffed with y'all's hollow-cheeked Halloween head

! Mama called the doctor ! and the doctor said:
No more monkeys jumping on the bed!!

———

(this is not about redemption)

MIND OVER MATTER

may simply be a discourse
        about the length and breadth
of the frail human body.

Its failed attempts to breathe
        something funereal. The desire
to step indelicately. A retreat

from language and
        December's patronizing wit.
It's conceivable that constant change –

in the absence of clear antecedents –
        hypothetically heightens the tension.
You see, most of what he thinks he knows is no more

than conjecture. He does remember
        C-rations, and something about
shell-casings appearing with a gospel

-like fervor in this intimate
        narrative of
unresolved dualism. Don't concern yourself

with what happened. So long as he keeps
        scabbing illusions of choice –
3x's a day with alprazolam – he can't complain.

THAT, MR DUBITO, is the wrong question ... (a circular poem)

What?

Now what?

Does it matter?

What's the matter?

What GOOD OL' DAYS?

Are we not blank slates?

WHAT were you thinking!?!

So what's your exit strategy?

That's what we have in common?

OMG! What is *wrong* with people?

WHAT has happened to *my world!?!*

*

WHO *am* I?

*

THAT, MR DUBITO, is the right question

(2) – SOMETHING'S HAPPENING HERE

Biden's Blunders : Russians : Coronavirus : Barr : Kobe Bryant : Stock Markets : Avenatti Amazon : Immigration : Taliban : Giuliani : Soleimani strike : EPA : CIA : GOP : FBI Thunberg : Zuckerberg : Obi wan Pompeo : rare ice balls on Lake Michigan : woman skinned in Mexico : Clarence Thomas talks : twin[!] Bomb Cyclones hammer Iceland Elon Musk - Falcon 9 : and lacking a coherent self, the President had people wondering

WHAT is the source code for all of your FUNCTIONS!?!

In a calming coronavirus press conference we heard reassuring comments like – *"we're almost all better now"*, and *"It's going to disappear. One day it's like a miracle, it will disappear[!]..."* in a manner that was reminiscent of the way pepper was used to mask the taste of rancid meat in the Middle Ages.

MEANWHILE: ImpeachablyPOTUS also made a brief appearance at the Daytona 500 [!] – *where his presidential motorcade drove on the track [whee!!]* – then raced to D.C. to attend the wedding of White House ghoul Stephen Miller at the Trump International. (Yes, the bride's dress was black.)

—

In photos, do you

wonder what was going on

beyond the frame's edge?

A BRIEF HISTORY OF ISOLATION: Quarantine

The cities remained, like numbered

Rocks piled at the seashore, mute

Testaments to an unpeopled landscape

Indifferent to the approaching sound of red

Handbells and the laughter of dead kings

A BRIEF HISTORY OF ISOLATION: At the local grocer's ...

the cashier asks
How are things?
and when I say, *Just ducky*
she stops & eyes me oddly, sez

What did you say?

So I say it again
Just ducky

Tipping her head, she leans toward
me now & in a hushed-voice
sez, *I used to work*
with prisons and
'just ducky'
was warden's code –
meant things were like
somebody's been stabbed
or
the prison was in lockdown

and I'm nodding
Yeah, like that...

NOSTALGIA: Philadelphia

We'd zigzag

past parentheses

of snow-swaddled

steaming homeless men

sleeping on sidewalks – where

even needle-heeled women were

forced to skirt the edges of despair

Cabbies would back up

one-way traffic – refuse to

move as car horns concatenated

like trapped slaughterhouse animals

queued in a cattle-chute gravid with doom

So much has changed – days

without actually seeing

anyone

even made ZOOM

seem almost normal

for a while ...

(... *you're on mute*)

SHOPPING

You're online shopping, but you're

Concerned your selections will seem

Arbitrary once you've seen them in your home

Liking a catalog of domestic moments

You'll register *polite* concern that

A Bluetooth beacon has been

Talking to your phone ...

Then notice reports of snow

In Los Angeles and

Begin scrolling

WOODED MOUNTAINS

Their habit of kneeling annoyed many

    and they didn't
    consider TikTok
    texting – or that story
    about wheat and weeds –
    reasons to teach
    about a dog with a bone . . .

They listened carefully
were not plagued with doubt
    and the dog
showed no surprise when they shot him

    What I'm trying to tell you is progressive
-ly unattractive, a product of a crude discontent depicting
fantasies of truth and a hatcheted reality awash in indifference

    – I stand in negativity –

The mythos is changeless : glorification of a gilded demagogue :
another absurd story about a *Tartuffe*-type turd (look it up!)
and the highly unlikely somedays he says will soon be here

So at some point you may have to decide which is better –
to live a lie in the culture of make-believe, or obtrude
upon the dusk in a chain of wooded mountains

      ————

Stock futures were mixed Monday as Wall Street anxiously awaited ...

OVID'S CLOWNS [*a conversation*]

☺ *Their design sense*
never overwhelms the image

       [There is – I'll grant you –
       careful composition in their array] ☺

☺ *They're enigmatic in the spotlight*
of symbolized complexions

       [But you must ask, are they just
       wildly inefficient decryption systems
       disrupting illusions of depth] ☹

☺ *Or are they more like pseudo*
-suicidal fools & quirky accidents
congregating in optimistic stories
of possessions & surroundings
luring and daring the senses to be
the sum of more than that which happens

       [Bah! That which *was*
       exists no more and that which *is*
       subsists in vacuous latitudes of baffling logic] ☹

☺ *But that which may yet be*
is ever-changing, like a comical circus routine
where an impossibly large number of clowns climb out of a small car

       [Yes! They *are* like slapstick visionaries
       whooping it up in the embarrassingly clueless
       riddle of human experience. What say you !?!] ☺

☺ *Methinks that*
by confronting our
collective desire to forget
they shame us into looking ...

CONGRESS: Libretto for a Clown Opera

(it's an *omnium-gatherum* of ignorants:
there's little they know how to do well)

- they lack the mental faculty or capacity for receiving & retaining facts
- they flout outrage, impaired integrity, & imitate things that matter
- they are like hungry, crazy people who throw away good food

Their presence their
Incessant dissents over
Time cultivate a mingled
Residue and strange unity
That elegies filter & realign
Inspired by dissimulation
Adding 3rd dimensions 2
Subvert any content that
Awakens/or arises from
   What-*ever*/wherever
Form and place appear
         ritualized
Putting 1 foot in front of the other
In public moments of unrequited
Expectations a wooly musky mix
Congress will inhale and whisk
All frothy into come to nothing
Deliberations even though they
Knew we was circlin' the drain

*   *

The libretto is (of course) recitative: the words are like eating garbage and drinking from gutters,
unaware of the telling signature of vomit-covered clothes (Yes, it's like Enkidu's dreams!!), but
we are reminded this is neither the story of a search for humanity nor the meaning of life.
NO!   This is about arrogance and hypocrisy … and the long still life of the dead.

A GOD-AWFUL SITUATION

It's disingenuous to complain
or question why we live like this

The unbearable illusion of choice
chokes the night with a clear intelligence

We bow our heads to sex guns and war
in the suffocating space of high testosterone

for We are but brittle membranes the *homeless* that
most spare schematic composition of jumbled figures

and They are content   spinimizing
the difference between Purpose and Meaning

Observe, these are not men of honor See
how they wriggle and squirm like clumsy demons

MR DUBITO's Predominant Symptomatology (at the Time of Evaluation)

Do you find it difficult to organize or keep track of your thinking?

Sometime yes life feels like optical delusion
Sometime is like shit-on-your-shoe or
make-believe story like postcard
from Witkiewicz only it's like
you've met your double
and marveled: *He.*
Might. Kill me!

Do other people say that it is difficult for you to stay on subject
or for them to understand you?

No that'd be fake news, like
defining good using bad
Sometime yes there's a
delayed reaction
but mostly it's
the thick scent of
violence & time-polished lies

Do you sometimes feel that other people are watching you
or talking about you?

In the time it takes
to turn & turn again
They perform benedictions
connecting doubt and brazenly
inflexible narrow notions of truth

*

Tell me, what more evidence do you require?

(3) – MIXED MESSAGING BEGINS

A man hosting a 'Corona' Party for 47 people in a New Jersey apartment was arrested

Denver reclassified its liquor stores as 'essential' after lines formed outside stores.

A man was arrested in Florida stealing 66 rolls of toilet paper from a hotel.

A man died after drinking fish tank cleaner to prevent coronavirus.

Obi wan Pompeo insisted the G7 adopt the term, "Wuhan Virus".

Citing *coronavirus*, the EPA suspended rules on monitoring and reporting pollution discharges and said it would not penalize companies that violated the existing rules. Our best hope for a better, cleaner world may be reduced to the possibility of parallel-selves living in quantum worlds where better versions of each one of us most certainly must exist.

— *we should be frightened of what we may become unless we're already all in Hell* —

Bonespurs declared himself our *'wartime president'* [said viewer ratings were up] then issued an order to reactivate retired and reserve troops to fight the coronavirus. Morgues were *at capacity* in New York. The Federal government (HHS) busily delivered non-functioning ventilators to California, and CISA – the Cybersecurity and Infrastructure Security Agency – designated *gun sellers* as part of the country's *"critical"* infrastructure during the coronavirus outbreak. Comments concerning US response efforts from various experts included ...

　　　　... When something happens, we throw a lot of money at it

　　　　... We were caught with our pants down

　　　　... Resources are constrained

　　　　... Extremely concerned

　　　　... This is unreal

　　　　　　Q: What is real?　　A: That which is irreplaceable.

MEANWHILE: POTUS continued his messaging: "*We must sacrifice together, because we are all in this together, and we will come through together. It's the invisible enemy. That's always the toughest enemy. But we are going to defeat the invisible enemy. I think we are going to do it even faster than we thought, and it'll be a complete victory. It'll be a total victory.*"　　　　... yup, the invisible enemy is always the toughest

If a river is busy moving

intangible determinants

with furious dedication

and a counterintuitive

choreography intervenes

beyond the intimate reach

of its personal narrative

you ought look to the

incorrect language

of our frenemies

to unlock the

why of how

we got

here

.

TABULA RASA: definitions (made clear)

Blank

(empty space)

Scraped tablet

(negation)

Existing in its original state

(ignorance)

An opportunity to start over w/o prejudice

(indifference)

A need or opportunity to start from the beginning

(trashed)

A situation in which nothing's yet been planned or decided

(interval)

The mind before it receives impressions gained from experience

(preoccupied)

DST: variations

You may be thinking, *DST? What the hell!?!* This is about how it makes you feel.
Did you wake up crabby? Disoriented? (At this point Fox News will not matter.)
Time-of-day suggests you should be hungry – but you're not. Washing last night's
dishes you wonder why you have so damn many clocks – then notice it snowed
overnight. Surveying the uppermost branches of a tree across the street triggers
a trio of rhyming *-ate* verbs ... *extricate ... exaggerate ... extrapolate ...*

I.   Drawn to light & shadow, my thoughts return to the first

signs of Spring – driving past a twilit copse of trees

bristling w/petulant crows – & how my vehicular attendance

lent cinematic substance to their incomprehensible confessions.

II.   Drawn to shadow & darkness, I circle back

to that same copse of twilit trees. Arguing with

ever-more-quarrelsome crows, I excoriate their incongruities

and blustering accusations with operatic richness.

III.   [Introduce a tangential incident to build on in order to advance

the preceding narrative.]

I remember wearing a black Def Leppard jacket that night – it was

chill! We'd gone to see La Bohème, but

there was something about the way the usher looked at us –

as if witnessing a murder

of squawking crows descending on a copse of trees.

[Now, socialize the following questions:

What do you think is going on here? What does DST mean?

Looking ahead, you'll need to ... (*excuse me – my head is calling*)

think of this this as an experiment.

No, this is not a punchline.

It is not a search for an epilogue.

It is not an example of creative indecision.

It is something else: how it ends is up to you.

There are universal truths & understandings to be had.

Write in a way where expectation will not determine outcome.]

(try again)

———

IIII.   You remember, don't you? We'd gone out for tapas after
La Boheme, and we were all wearing black – like poets! Our server *heaved*
a sigh as we were being seated – said *OMG!*
Don't you just hate Daylight Savings!?!
Then suddenly sunny
she introduced herself, winked and – by way
of a devilishly engaging stage-whisper – inquired
So, are you guys somebody?

———

*

CONTINUITIES: Time, shadows, darkness & light

                                  – uncertain memories of La Boheme –

                                  the operatic imagery of screeching poets & crows.

CASE STUDIES: The changing of our clocks

                                  precipitates a misalignment with our bodies'

                                  natural rhythms and may set in motion

                                  increased risk of heart attack.

                                  (*The extended evening light*

                                             delays the brain's release of melatonin.)

TEACHABLE MOMENT: The portion of the brain

                                       that manages circadian rhythms

                                                 is located in the hypothalamus.

APPLICATIONS: (general)   Perched like a coal-black bird, another

                                     part of the brain aligns the tongue

with its uncertainties. When

                                  your mother dies you'll think

of twenty questions. To acquire the artfulness

                                  required to humanize her, jot them down.

APPLICATIONS: (specific)   Soon you will meet a certain POET. Do not trust him.

Do *NOT* spit on his tongue, for it is written:

"*Poets are talking crows in human form.*"

*

        As we became more aware
of his pitch-perfect talent, we gathered
        every thing for which we had no name
but ushered forth from him
        like wind before the rain –
pig : stick : fire/fish/gourd
        and the firmness of our growing
reverence had the air of being unshakeable –
        until blunt-force trauma
demanded to be defined, followed by
        bludgeoned/brutalized/gang-raped/and murdered ...
gypsy bands of homeless words, desperate
        for description, trailblazed their way through his mind

He woke up covered
        in excrement & vomit. This is the point at which
he first got wind of Dogma. Lacking a foundation for our beliefs
        we could have ended up like humpback whales
postulating about tigers on the moon, or been galvanized
        by the countless Cumaean prophecies set forth
in that classic celestial saga about an incorrigible
        orange dog indulging the urge to gorge on its own tail

        trust me ...

This is why we have Dogma and little use for poets

    This is why there are no tigers on the moon

TALKING THE HIND LEGS OFF A DONKEY

If the act of forgetting is an empty intention
        is a memory gap like a child in a well

                My neighbor makes me think
                that struggles to stay on topic are
                not all that unique as I listen to twaddle
                about squash vines, a philandering father-in
                -law, & an extensive genealogy search going back
                a thousand years revealing a *y*-marker from Ireland
                and a surprise '*lass*' from France (*how did that happen?*)
                His tongue-wagging takes a turn Now he's prattling about
                how I bear a striking resemblance to a [dead] Slavic friend

                        – my head begins to hurt –

Conversations can be like this – random as a meteor shower
Fleetingly, thoughtlessly entering our personal atmospheres

                My therapist doesn't tell me I
                need to move on, that the past
                is the past because it's made up
                of who and what we were and R
                that there is no Here and Now –
                the Theory of Light suggests that
                what we are looking at may not be
                what we can even agree to believe
                just happened ... *uncertainty* is the
                constant gardener of reinterpretation
                propagating in provinces of possibility

                And now I'm the one rambling
                w/no logical or meaningful connection
                BTW! Can somebody tell me ... Was anyone able
                to rescue the little blind girl, the one that fell into the well

ONE THING LED TO ANOTHER

The plain-spoken poet was lyin'

spreadeagled at the bottom of a stairwell.

No stranger to primitive tensions, the cages tell him

this is a gibbeting place, a reminder

of what happens to people who think

free will exempts them from unwritten rules.

       There are shouts for a rope

the stairwell goes black ... survival mode kicks in

fight or flight/someone strikes an Ohio Blue Tip!

Cursing Apollo, the poet thinks – *not this again* –

as his fluttering heartbeat naturally quickens

materializing in a shapeshift of black feathers & wings

designed for the improvisatory resurrection of talking crows.

CROW

Staring into the sun
    with ripple-less optimism.

Devouring black
    in counterintuitive narratives.

Ethereal urgencies radiate
    from its infinitely nuanced feathering.

As the crow sings, a sightless child emerges from a well –
    "Certainly what I'm hearing must be a murder!"

With much effort the crow responds:
    "Spit on my tongue."

(4) — ALTERNATE REALITIES

Rare leatherback sea turtles built nests on empty Thailand tourist beaches during the coronavirus partial national lockdown.

British primatologist and conservationist Jane Goodall said that she hoped a global movement of people calling for clean air would result from the global coronavirus outbreak, which emptied cities of traffic.

Social distancing guidelines were now being recommended for family pets in the U.S.

PETA pressured the Pentagon to halt drinking cobra blood and killing animals in survival training.

And we speculated that pangolins, not snakes, may have been the missing link for transmission of the new coronavirus from bats to humans.

The U.S. death toll passed 60,000 by April's end, a number that Trump had predicted the U.S. would not exceed. But *he* didn't expect a second wave of the coronavirus in the fall. And *if* a second wave *were* to occur, he said it would be mere *"embers"* of infection that could be *easily* snuffed out.

At a Coronavirus Task Force Briefing, the Tiny-fisted Emperor said, "*Supposing we hit the body with a tremendous, whether it's ultraviolet or just very powerful light ... Supposing you brought the light inside the body, which you can do, either through the skin or in some other way ... Then I see the disinfectant where it knocks it out in one minute. Is there a way we can do something like that, by injection inside, or almost a cleaning*?"

He also said he expected the warmer temperatures and sunny days of summer to contain its spread. Dr. Anthony Fauci added he'd like to agree with the president – but then they'd both be wrong.

With more than one million COVID-19 cases confirmed in the US, Jared Kushner called the coronavirus crisis *"a great success story."* *"We've achieved all the different milestones that are needed. The federal government rose to the challenge."*

> *setting, viewpoint, theme, and rhythm*
> *reduced to vague abstractions in*
> *an improbable, pitiless play*
>
> *inchoate lines steeped in contradictions*
> *play fast and loose with maledictions, but*
> *COVID does not one day, magically just go away*

DREAM INTERPRETATION: Oracle

THE DREAM:

I see a city of wood.　　　Lacking fixedness　　　　　it moves

in the wind like a sinister forest infused with old adjectives.

I wear a conjugated hoody; it has a metabolism.

That it provides distressing episodes

of dissociation is a given.

I carry

a dictionary:

It is the *Dictionnaire
Philosophique Portatif.*

My life feels like an immoderate search

for a box of Ohio Blue Tips

and a can of gasoline.

It is a fidgety – *'Runs with Scissors!'* – way of life.

───────────

ORACLE:

*This is about the Divine Fire that burns within
and the Concepts of Knowledge and Destruction.*

DREAMING of Dos Passos

Adorned in the lusty black and red of anarchy

he searches for a habit-ruled monastery to purge his fever dreams

    'Ernest and I used to read the Bible to each other'

Well-established in the exchange of guns, metal weapons, and captives

he arrives in Madrid expecting to meet his old friend, José Robles

    'Come, and bring a lot of drunks'... he scribbles

My avocation, he avers, is the incendiary test of institutions

Removing a glove he lights a match: *'Being Everyman*

                    is a lonely, ruthless quest!!'

The match goes out, but by cockcrow nothing remains of the abbey

LIVIN' THE DREAM

I never changed...Come hunt me, ancient friend, and tell me I am wrong.
John Berryman - The Dream Songs: #259

The universe suggests parallel lives
may be like postcards from Witkiewicz
And if I have mentioned this before, well ...

A pivot of apostrophes when little's left –
  I thought it was comin', the breakdown
The occasional indecisive cursive detour –
  Women of god see me and run
That eloquent sense of barely-thereness –
  I been away thutty years

Now you understand my need to more fully consider this particular
juncture of life's journey having realized maybe I need to pay more
attention to the ripples the impending end of mortality/reality and
seriously with some sort of endgame in mind/it's like it's almost the
end of summer and you haven't watered in a while – but you're still
expecting flowers [!] In another place it would be like sitting outside
on an early-August evening & noticing a glass of Chardonnay seems
to be sweating *way* beyond what's normal and serves up a reminder
that you may not have too much more time best not be foolin' around

  I had a psychiatrist
  I'm glad I met him
    but he never helped me none

... In the deciphered disequilibrium – a hand-scrawled experience

  I am not without sentiment ... it's just
  that throughout nights long and still
  I remain a restless story

... In the jagged-edged details – trees, civilizations   life

  Ancient friends came back to haunt me
  They found me changed
    but I was not wrong

... And (*things being what they are*) I now find myself in this
"cardboard condition", which is why I've simply written ...

ANYTHING HELPS
THANKS AND GOD BLESS!

BOUNDARIES

if   like disembodied prepositions
            tireless attempts to be content
do not serve you and you're finding time

        and its collaborators
                difficult to contain
        maybe you've already asked

how can we stop the reconceived past
        from marrying the dread the
unconventional manner in which night comes out of hiding

        maybe it's time you consider why
                what collectively amounts to blah-blah blah
        means everything is up for grabs :

coal mines : uranium : anything for profit : proxy wars :
blacks in prison : gang-raped women : compassionate
        conservatives : misogynist religions :

        child abuse :

        trafficking . . .

        one could even say

        our inescapable acculturation
            has taught us to be tacit – like
        the Dancing Boys of Afghanistan

        whose circumstance is defined
                by irrefragable boundaries –
        the fuckers : and the fucked

HEADSPACE

In a sea of sunflowers
there are circumstances where
you may find you're hanging on to a
splotch of red, and this is the very reason
you need to take some time, some time to think –

look
to the Chilean
desert to deliver you
from the split tongue of hope

Back in a stark red place
when you try to recall the
details, the composite image
may now insist upon including

a second person from a rural
property who raises questions
about your inhumanity, whether
the two of you can coexist, but it is

by this you will be reminded
of how the rhythm of a line
penned by an unseen hand
first revealed itself – you *could*
ask, *Is there no room for dissent*
within your certainties – Instead

say, *Ya' know, with the exception of blue*
Rimbaud got it wrong too; then put into
plain words the unassailable color of vowels –
White *I*, Yellow *A*, Red *E*, Blue *O*, Black *U* –

White – is for Savorless Psalms
Yellow – honors Cold Vomit and the Madness of van Gogh
Red – as you might expect, fulfills our Sanguinary Needs
Blue – pertains to the Nimbus of Saints, and
Black – Black was always about Raptus, Lust, Rimbaud & Verlaine

Rimbaud famously wrote: "A noir, E blanc, I rouge, U vert, O bleu : voyelles"

SURRENDER

The illusion of the soul and the biblical
Balm of suffering frame the abbot's despair like
Infected metaphors. Against all logic he
Thinks - why I am here cannot be reconciled with
This ghoulish diorama of phallocentric
History, or the attitudes, fears, and desires
Found in the many versions of morality.
Like notes from a dark cello, doubt descends the
Staircase of his mind to confront Will, Choices, and
The lesser-known battlefield of Fatalism

Where to be ill-informed becomes necessary
When no clear story emerges to move us past
Morose repetition. Thus, where a samurai
Would choose death, the monk gives ground to Vanity.

RING OF FIRE

Crossing the sunny plaza, she is bathed in the warm orange of improper nouns
Castrated memories portray the way she walks as an act of wickedness
Cluttered geometries detail the indefinable way she moves

:: our scribe translates the condemnation ::

unbound by the nature of necrotized verbs
so shall all men mark the way of sin when seen
for now and for all ~ it is written

:: then thinks to himself ::

The isolated and time-deprived
hunger for comfort ... the
wisdom of the grave
-side visitors, and visions
of the life that could have been, should
by now, have put right what we wish for

Instead, we fill the emptiness with
religious fervor and rat-riddled rage

:: Indiscernibly, our scribe squirms
then appends the condemnation ::

Forever, have I dreamt of the Ring of Fire
and the sensuous curvature of a lateen sail
filled with delight, as it apprehends the wind

:: setting aside his pen, Mr Dubito absents himself and ...
but that's another story ::

Bygone

barefoot passions

reside in sympathetic hearts

Age will do this – smiling at trysts with

Reason & Spirit, as if it is not like

anything that could possibly

have happened before

In spite of whatever else

you may believe, it's not a gift

knowing the recondite concords and

discords of clock and calendar, this

arabesque of time, and the long

long sleep that awaits, is all

anyone ever really has

(5) — NEW BEGINNINGS [pt.1]

Trump revised his estimated coronavirus death toll for the fifth time in two weeks: "*I used to say 65,000 and now I'm saying 80 or 90 and it goes up and it goes up rapidly.*" He went on to praise himself for solving "*every problem*" and taking care of "*all of the things.*"

Not quite done, standing in front of stacked boxes of medical supplies in Allentown, Pennsylvania, the Leader of the Free World said that frontline nurses and doctors "*running into death just like soldiers run into bullets*" is "*a beautiful thing to see.*"

MEANWHILE: as the U.S. approached 100,000 coronavirus-related deaths in the first 100 days of the pandemic, it's rumored that Trumpty Dumpty has privately vowed to continue his unceasing efforts to wish away the virus.

(5) — NEW BEGINNINGS [pt.2]

Then Blursday, May 25th happened, and *everything* went to hell: the country erupted in protest over the death of George Floyd.

POTUS responded to this pivotal national moment by tweeting threats about how to handle protesters demonstrating in front of the White House.

— [with "*vicious dogs*" and "*most ominous weapons*"] —

A CNN reporter and his camera crew were arrested while filming the rioting on live TV in Minneapolis : A local Louisville, Kentucky reporter and a camera operator were shot with pepper balls by police in the middle of a live broadcast covering protests against police brutality : Atlanta set a curfew : Milwaukee imposed a curfew : Violent protests erupted in Brooklyn : Police and protesters clashed in Detroit : Protesters marched in downtown Miami : Protestors & police clashed in Los Angeles : Denver announced a city-wide nightly curfew : Vandalism and looting rocked the city of Portland.

Violent protests are not the story here. Police violence is. With pardons, abdication of oversight, harsh rhetoric, and executive orders, the Trump administration had basically encouraged police violence against Black Americans. George Floyd's killing opened the wounds of centuries of American racism.

— Trump Facts —

— Trump claimed he'd done more for the Black community than any president since Lincoln —

MR DUBITO'S FAVORITE TIME OF DAY

His dreams often play out in a less demanding time
      (before we started punching flight attendants)
Back when travel was almost a fantasy, not
      something to be endured
Between departure and destination, back
      when '*expressways*' actually were, and smoking
KOOL cigarettes was still cool/ but on the periphery of his

Idealities, a hellfire has burst forth – an Inferno befouls the air ::
      grey & orange-ish brown – creating indistinct images with
Lingering fetidities/akin to sitting by an open window on a
      city bus/suffocatingly behind a garbage truck, and
Like a simmering slow-cooker at a Cajun-BBQ, it's pungency is

Everywhere following an unabated week of high 90's heat/so it's
      understandable that his spidey-sense is also all a-tingle/'bout
Climate change/what it might be like (*cuz this sure as shit ain't normal*)

      Where does one begin/ How
    do we reconcile the gardens of the past
   with the indiscriminate actions of the present

Upon waking he thinks: *This has always been my favorite time of day*
      – the incoherent hour before sunrise –
    When everything is still
      unsubstantial, and open to debate

FILLING IN THE BLANKS

(temporarily holding back)

        We were making paper cranes

        Plans for summer

           Next thing I knew

        we no longer had a common language –

              I had no clue: no map: no plan

(speeding up)

        I asked, how could anyone

        have incontrovertible knowledge

          of what is Real vs Conceptual

        once the power of suggestion commences

              seeding the subconscious mind ...

(slightly slower)

        ... To that, you can readily imagine others saying:

          – *Yeah, I'm sorry, he's lost his mind* –

              (I did look, and at times it did seem like

           some important things were nowhere to be found)

(faster now)

          You tell yourself, Wait! *What?*

(free adjustment of tempo)

        And maybe that wasn't how it happened ...

          you know how insufficient

        mental confabulations can be

              ——

(gradually slowing down)

        In time to come, by way of explanation, I was assured

         : *the information you seek is in the universe* :

           in a - *memory is a fragile construct*

             kind of conversation

KABUKI

Jogging your memory   something has put you in mind of
          Chianti bottles wrapped in straw   you know the kind
repurposed as *ristorante* type candle holders

heavy with beaded wax   collected from countless
          cheap colored candles and how our guests appeared
charmed when we'd explain the *fiasco's* were all but self-decorating

(we are so done with decorating)   Rather than making another
          exhausting entry in a diary of dashed hopes & dreams –
without planning to – you start writing about candlewax ...

          ... and there it is – and it feels like
                    the willing suspension of disbelief
                              on the stage of a tactless Kabuki play

                    where the actors
               clearly fail to realize
          that personal tone

and the ongoing resistance to punctuation
          are duty-bound to mindlessly amplify remorse
-less episodes of petty domestic squabbles

MR DUBITO SEZ

My wallpaper and I
are not fighting because
in the end no one will
escape this narrative
of blurred uncertainties
arranged like a sentence
to a disquieting
prison A time-capsule
of stories that have not
aged well Tell me my friend
what is the difference
between the future and
deconstructing the past

SAME: but different

TWITTER :: X

Vagrants :: Unhoused

The Spanish Flu :: COVID-19

Hunter Gatherer :: Hunter Biden

Roget's Thesaurus :: wordhippo.com

Barf Bag :: Motion Discomfort Receptacle

Explosion :: Rapid Unscheduled Disassembly

"Moby Dick" :: "Zoey Punches the Future in the Dick"

Encyclopedia Britannica :: Google – WIKIPEDIA – FACEBOOK

Unidentified Flying Object :: Unidentified Anomalous Phenomenon

Shell Shock :: Combat-Related Post-Traumatic Stress Disorder (PTSD)

"On the Origin of Species" :: "Hurricane Lizards and Plastic Squid"

The Soviet Union: (USSR) :: The Russian Federation (Rossiya)

"Maria Beetle" – the book :: "Bullet Train" – the movie

New Deal – Roosevelt :: Art of the Deal – Trump

Lyndon Baines Johnson :: MAGA Mike Johnson

Her Story :: ~~ROE v WADE~~ :: History

A BRIEF HISTORY OF ISOLATION: The adjustments ...

were

without

end We

worked

from our

homes, then

came the layoffs

wildfires, storms, the

constant political unrest

& homeschooling ... in the end

struggling to provide even basic needs

was overwhelming Sometimes we'd

find mom sitting on the toilet

just staring at a wall

MAGA

Was it just

One hundred years ago

That we were great

A time when you could

Lynch a Black man simply

Because he was Black

Or his wife had uttered

– *unwise remarks* –

Maybe

It's more recent

Someplace where '*Driving*

While Black' might get you

Beaten with a flashlight or

Incentivize you to shove

15-yards of toilet paper

Down your own throat

A short while after

Being pepper-sprayed

Taken into custody, but

That's still not a broad enough definition

Is it   Because in The Opera of Subjectivity

You must also take this for granted: that *their*

Dramatis personae are reading from an entirely

Different kind of libretto, one that does *not* declare

We are all free – *Just shoot them – crack their skulls* –

We hold these truths to be self-evident

~~Excessive~~ use of force by law enforcement is an unusual but at times necessary aspect of ~~racial unrest~~ arrest

STUDY LIST

[from which may be learned: *you so do not have a glass of wine if all that's left is the spider*]

(*)

we think it's reasonable to expect people will capably reflect social values
electing leaders is a *charade*, a somber counterpoint to razor-topped fencing
people try to be *authentic* in blank spaces that do not allow for deep reflection
porcelain insights camouflage the intuitive aspects of being *murder machines*
the restroom's metal door has ~~shit~~ scratched on one side *FUCK* on the other
how do I know this infinite, improbable universe is not all in my head!?!
we think we can think about things with *a quality of oblique reserve*
this is not about *trafficking* women & children, or internal organs
we fear cultural homogenization *and* people that are different
this is not about the Internet of Things *or* morbid obesity
this is not about *the prevalence* of *partner violence*
this is not about a *dysfunctional* government
this is not about *poverty and racism*
this is not about *life* on Mars
this is not about being
the *sum* of chemical
compounds, or
drops of rain
in a river
serving as
metaphors
for all those
that have lived
and died; this is
about the dismembered
language of silence in times
of social unrest, the ambiguity of
memory, and the festival of ignorance

(repeat)

GHOSTS OF JIM HARRISON

I was a dog on a short chain
and now there's no chain.

Jim Harrison, "Barking"

Standing before The Gates of Hell – at the Rodin Museum in Philadelphia –

you say you can see Pripyat (the Ghost City) with your blinded eye.

Michigan's Upper Peninsula – an unfortunate step

disturbs an underground Vespula nest the size of a basketball.

Chased by swarming yellowjackets, you parkour to the Iron River.

In the shade of a row of Gingko trees just outside Kyoto – squatting

w/a woodcarver – coaxing a one-eyed Buddha from a block of wood.

Picking your way into the Sonoran Desert.   Crossing an arroyo

you catch sight of Mr Dubito descending a steep embankment.

Smiling broadly, you wave and shout ... *Well, Come On!!*

* * *

Juneteenth was the oldest nationally celebrated commemoration of the ending of slavery in the United States. Forty-seven states and the District of Columbia marked June 19 as a state holiday or observance. Communities across the country celebrated it with food & festivities. But – despite a push by activists over the years – Juneteenth would not be recognized as a federal holiday until 2021, when President Joe Biden designated June 19 as Freedom Day.

(6) – REARRANGING DECK CHAIRS ON THE TITANIC

Most agreed that these times were truly Loony Toons. Whether removed or toppled, statues of bigots, racists, and Civil War era 'heroes' were finally coming down. Displaying the Confederate flag was banned by the nation's military and *NASCAR* in the same week. Trump's thoughtless tough-guy tweets seemed increasingly out-of-step with current events and, well, everywhere in general. Fondly recalling the protests in Minneapolis, Trump heralded the use of tear gas and other force to disperse protesters, calling it a *"beautiful scene"*; he openly enthused about the National Guard's actions saying they were *"like a knife cutting butter."*

MEANWHILE: The Republican National Committee announced it was relocating its August convention from Charlotte, NC to Jacksonville FL after Gov. Roy Cooper said he would require the convention to be downsized due to COVID-19. Florida Governor Ron DeSantis and Jacksonville Mayor Lenny Curry jumped in and said they'd *welcome!* crowds of 50,000 people. So, Trump's perfect presidential renomination event was then re-scheduled to take place on the 60th anniversary of Jacksonville's "Ax Handle Saturday" where civil rights protesters – staging a sit-in protest against racial segregation at a "whites-only" lunch counter – had been attacked by a local KKK mob.

(The in-person convention would be canceled a month later due to Florida's coronavirus surge.)

MEANWHILE: Trump downplayed the latest spikes in COVID-19 cases saying, *"If we stop testing right now, we'd have very few cases, if any."* *"Instead of 25 million tests, let's say we did 10 million tests. We'd look like we were doing much better because we'd have far fewer cases. You understand that."*   Umm, no.

MEANWHILE: Despite the record spike in COVID-19 cases the Administration moved forward to *end* Federal support for testing sites *and had yet to distribute nearly $14 billion* intended to help state and local governments improve coronavirus testing and contact tracing.

Dept of Don't Worry, Be Happy: At the first White House coronavirus task force briefing held in *two months*, Cheerleader Pence was all, *"We slowed the spread, we flattened the curve, we saved lives."* *"We're in a much better place…"*

– Global Coronavirus Deaths Neared 500,000 As The Number Of Cases Surpassed 10 Million –

"And we have an election coming up this fall."

NEIGHBORS: June …

[*And no, Mr Rogers did not adequately prepare me for the people in my neighborhood*]

We/I have a new neighbor

full-lipped/striking – Kafkaesque

tattoos zhooshing a coquettish demeanor –

a woman who

looks like she/

they may well be

in witness-protection

or involved in a

messy relationship

with a Russian gangster …

Another neighbor I occasionally see

sees me sitting out on my patio, sez …

Hi, you doin' all right … ?

then spit-launches into a narrative re

-capitulating villainies she has suffered in

her ongoing spat with the local condo association

FRUSTRATED, Stacey sez

I get it, I know

they're saying

– EFF YOU –

but these are WHITE WOMEN!

(I have *no* idea what she's talking about)

Then, in passing, she sez she is *so, so pleased* to learn the

wrecked car she saw was not mine in her : *hello, I must be going* : kind of way

MIDNIGHT RAIN

Now we will count to twelve and let's keep quiet

-- Pablo Neruda

When I counted to 12

no apostle came to mind – just

a cardinal number where the infinite

set of N = {good cop/bad cop, wolf + crow ... }

A desultory stone stillness

confronts the poet

within the informal borderline

of another rhyme

-less midnight

In the distance – unhurried lightning –

ghost mountains in silhouette ...

It's not raining where I am, yet, but it will be soon

BAD DREAM

Dreaming of the Cumaean Sibyl
Mr Dubito listens as she purrs
nightmarish news of chill & dread – cocooning
her chicanery in cryptic uncertainty, she
tarries in the pivot & slur of murky visions
festooned with bones and viscera

Haltingly / she predicts a near future / accoutered in un
-familiar fabrics / tailored / plying other-worldly patterns /
  :: *Scissored! / in the Hands of an Angry God!* ::

(*still dreaming, Mr Dubito absorbs her vaguely dire warnings, sez*)

You speak as though life had some purpose
Life is a baleful abstract with abstruse annotations
hollow as colloquies with dead Czars or ancient Caesars

Consider : what is significant vs what we do : why
would anyone put their trust in you : we're just
deposits in the dark humus of closed systems
disciples of meaningless work

    – Here the dream ends –

    Half-asleep/Half-awake
    Mr Dubito rolls onto his side

– a train whistle wails, insistent and cheerless –

    and as it begins to rain, he thinks
        "Après moi, le déluge"

    but he does not go back to sleep

GHOSTS IN THE MACHINE

'And If the Nature of Thought Is Not Everywhere the Same' ...

CHOICES – delusional explanations of poor decisions
AGAIN – unreconciled frenzy
ROSY – garish surrogates; distorted spiritual consciousness

THE CLAPPERED MUSIC OF HOODED LEPERS

DARK – a Russian texture of language
POLITICS – embarrassed narratives of complicity, like dry coitus
AMBIGUITY – contradictory pronouncements and phrases

IT TAKES TIME TO BURN A VILLAGE PROPERLY

DEPRESSION – damaged imagination
INKBLOT – a disturbingly vulgar stain
GIBBERISH – mangled themes of unrest

TO NOT FEEL LIKE MYSELF TO BE BESIDE MYSELF I'M NOT MYSELF TODAY

So, how are you feeling, otherwise?
I'm just not myself today.

Can you describe what you're feeling?
My emotional range is pretty much limited
to anger and paralyzing anxiety.

Do you want to talk about it?
That's why I'm here.

Our time is almost up, but tell me, is what you're feeling something new?
Let's talk about this next time.
'Now' feels like we're veering toward awkward (...)

SERMONS – ponderous theorizing in a wild mix of styles
THOUGHTS – desperately ineffectual persuasion of sublime awareness
ZEN – deeply troubled grotesqueries of poverty; unassuageable whimsy

* * *

Abelard said,

'The beginning of wisdom is found in doubting; by doubting
we come to the question, and by seeking
we may come upon the truth.'

So, I asked my therapist why

      silent moments retain the eloquence of an autopsy

why a catalog of losses

      seeking balance in the heavy gravity of self-reflexive moments

uncomfortably reprograms memory at the expense of feeling

      and why does this line of thinking become lost

in man-made noise lost

      in the reek of human flesh lost

in the dense smell of ammonia as the body burns muscle

LIFELESS — the smile of an executioner
MISTRUST — de-emphasized relationships
RUINS — rubble from exaggerated perspectives

* * *

She said,

    Have you asked yourself why you stood in line for this?

* * *

BLU-82

Born and raised in PATHOLOPOLIS

The BLU-82 'Daisy Cutter' was a 15,000 pound, parachute-launched bomb

we thought and spoke easily in a homicidal language

Designed to detonate just above ground, it generated overpressures
of a thousand pounds per square inch in a three mile kill zone

absolving the aftermaths like followers of Leibniz or disciples of Pope

Survivors were provided with great psychological punishment
as they began to bleed from eyes, nose, and ears

in this best of all possible worlds.

... AT NEVER BEFORE SEEN LEVELS

(a circular poem)

Covid in Houston wastewater was ... _____

The national debt is rising ... _____

Lake Mead is drying up and is currently ... _____

Experts feared student loan defaults would be ... _____

Virginity testing on women and children is ... _____

Child stunting in Syria could be ... _____

The transgender population is growing ... _____

Atmospheric CO2 is ... _____

Arctic temperatures are ... _____

Smurfing is ... _____

Anxiety and stress are ... _____

The teacher shortage is ... _____

Violence and trauma are ... _____

Antisemitism is ... _____

Housing prices are ... _____

Microbial diversity was ... _____

We're seeing the universe ... _____

Suspected terrorists could cross borders ... _____

Trump accused the FBI and DOJ of leaking ... _____

They're willing to use prosecutorial misconduct ... _____

There is unprecedented use of the phrase ... _____

Mr Dubito was trying to convince

Himself, that this stretch of West Michigan

Weather – bein' in the 90's – wasn't really remarkable

But it was … it was the 3rd week in June and

The "Wettest Winter - Driest Spring"

On record had just ended

*

He'd thought the

Hens & Chicks would thrive

Or at least survive these conditions

But they didn't, and while he was taking some

Soil samples, an astonishingly zombie-looking Hen left him

Bleeding, stabbed by the prickle now protruding from his thumb

OWW!! (Pay Attention: *point taken, lesson learned*) – Stunned

He thought, *GEEZ! When's the last time I even had a sliver?*

Looking around he sees the Peonies are steaming –

Solomon's Seal looks scraggly – of remaining

Bleeding Hearts, there is but one …

His thumb begins throbbing

*

Even so, by 8, Mr Dubito is

channel surfing HEADLINE NEWS …

* Cruelty to Animals * Voting in Florida *

* Illegal Deportations * Human Trafficking *

* Inflation * Pink Eye * Early Onset Dementia *

hovering like a hawk, he coolly blinks & zeros in on

* The Most Gangster Enchiladas in Albuquerque, NM *

(7) – TANGLED CLUSTERS OF DOUBT

COVID-19: Global total confirmed cases: 11,353,190; Total deaths: 530,858
U.S. Total confirmed cases: 2,856,414; Total deaths: 129,730

Recent guidance from the White House on the continuing spike in the number of cases: Americans need to learn to *"live with the virus being a threat."*

Wait, what happened to…*"the problem goes away in April"*; *"packed churches all over our country"* on Easter Sunday; *"by Memorial Day weekend we will have this coronavirus epidemic behind us"*; the country will be *"really rocking again"* by July.

The World Health Organization acknowledged there was emerging evidence that the coronavirus could be spread by *leedle, teeny, tiny particles suspended in the air.* Imagine that. Meanwhile, Trump formally began the U.S. withdrawal from the World Health Organization amid a 1-day coronavirus case record for the *nth* time in *x*_days.

Singing *"Hands up, please don't shoot me"* - a 'Wall of Moms,' wearing bike helmets & goggles, gathered each night in Portland to link arms and form a protective barrier between law enforcement and Black Lives Matter protesters.

Trump Facts – On cognitive testing: *"I actually took one when I - very recently, when I when I was - the radical left were saying, is he all there? Is he all there? And I proved I was all there, because I got - I aced it. I aced the test."*

"Americans and British have different ways of saying things. They say 'elevator,' we say 'lift' … they say 'President,' we say 'stupid psychopathic git.'"   …Alexei Sayle

Dept. of - This Again, Really? Trump kept insisting that the cognitive test he recently took was [really, really] *"difficult"* and *"not that easy"* because he had to correctly recall the phrase *"Person. Woman. Man. Camera. TV."* Dr. Ziad Nasreddine, the doctor who developed the 10-minute Montreal Cognitive Assessment (MoCA) examination said, *"it's supposed to be easy,"*…   unless you're cognitively impaired.

Saying he was *"very impressed"*, POTUS re-tweeted tweets from Dr. Stella Immanuel advocating for hydroxychloroquine, who in the past also said gynecological problems are caused by individuals having sex with demons and witches in their dreams.

In unrelated Trump news, First Lady ~~Malaria~~ Melania Trump announced plans to renovate and update the iconic Rose Garden with improved drainage, new flowers and plants, new support for television appearances, and better accessibility for those with disabilities. Tear gas and flash grenades were not mentioned.

CLEMENCY

Speaking with the voice of Peter – Servant

of the servants of God – Christ's vicar approved

"The Index of Forbidden Books" in 1559

the influence of which is understated.

Burned on a pyre along with his copy of

Voltaire's "Philosophical Dictionary"

consider a young Chevalier's arrest

for *'wearing his hat while a church procession passed'*

and *'for the singing of blasphemous songs'*.

Voltaire pleads to the French Parliament to spare

the life of François-Jean de la Barre: ears and

right hand cut off, tongue torn out, sentenced to hang –

the clergy demand death by the stake – then yield

and allow that first he may be beheaded.

* * *

[François-Jean de la Barre (12 September 1745 – 1 July 1766) was a young French nobleman, and the last person executed for blasphemy in France.]

MOTHERS

(COVERUPS)

The oil companies knew. The car companies knew.

Chemical & tobacco companies – yup, they all knew too.

And the government? *Pleez*. You knew they'd pull a fast one.

(ILLEGALS)

Yeah – *Boo Hoo, that's a pity* – to their uncertain situation:

Pack them muthas on a bus & send 'em to some woke city!

Was how border bureaucrats masterminded immigration.

(AFFECTION)

My aunt said

Smothering her mother

Was the most difficult thing she'd ever done.

THE NEIGHBOR'S WIFE

Seeing her, I would find myself musing about
comfortless operas, replete with pole-dancers
in sollerets, behaving like cheerless angels
fond of mawkish hissing at suppositious sins.
I felt sick as a parrot when I saw her trip
her husband down their walk-up steps! I kept blinking
(*can't believe it!!*) turning away, then back again –
like Cezanne's doubt – the scene not seen the same way twice:
an ambulance arrived, then a delivery
car – with carry-outs [!] ... it was a bit after that

that neighbors up and down the street rearranged their
curtains and came scurrying out of their homes to
brush up on stories about *her* & *what's-his-name*
and speculate about the order they'd sent away.

The neighbor called him over –

pointing, she said,   *Look!*

    Baby rabbits!

He walked back to his shed

returned with a square mouth

shovel and using the flat of the blade

banged 3 kits in the head, but a 4th ran off

squealing giving rise to Dad snarling–

    STEP ON HIM!!

But she just stood there, he said –

didn't say a word

she just stood there

OF COURSE

Mom once asked my father – was he

surprised that I was writing poetry

My father said – of course

he writes poetry –

he's my son.

NEIGHBORS: July ...

Lured by the promise of an evening in the mid-70's

I'm on the patio settling in as the neighborhood dogs

begin offering up opinions from their corner of the world

and for some reason I think of a young fireman in Detroit who

was our next-door neighbor, rescuer of two Rottweiler pups that

after a time   he would come to chain to a stud in his garage when

at work, which   when they were pups no more   they ripped away

from the wall, chewed through the siding, and jumped the adjoining

fence, to land in *our* yard with our two-year old daughter – not long

after that, the *situation* resolved itself, or so we thought when we

were no longer aware of the dogs for days, which soon became

weeks – some months later, the neighbor on the other side

of the fireman's home, casually, one evening over drinks

told us how much this incident had bothered her

and   being a prison nurse   how she had access

to a number of *expired* drugs she'd seasoned

a couple of steaks with ...   before tossing

them over her fence into the next yard

gradually refashioning that evening's

feeding frenzy to what surely must

have been the same starless hush

we were suddenly experiencing

———

Next thing I knew

it was August

(8) – A LINGERING AFTERTASTE WITH AN UNPLEASANT BITE

The 1ST Sunday in August encouraged us to enjoy waning summer rays with those dearest to us

Sunday: 8/2/2020 – ~~HOW TO OBSERVE AMERICAN FAMILY DAY~~ – (*cancelled due to* COVID)

~~Tour a museum. Take an art class together. Pick up some fresh fruit together. Play games outdoors~~ or ~~go for a walk. Visit grandparents and bring them a picnic lunch.~~

AUGUST 2nd IS ALSO NATIONAL COLORING BOOK DAY!

During COVID, National Coloring Book Day recognizes the joy children *and* adults alike derive from coloring in pages of designs. When someone visits, be sure to leave a coloring book and crayons or coloring pencils in the guest room to use while they're being quarantined.

Amid growing concerns about the extended first wave of the coronavirus and the looming threat of the second wave later this fall and winter, Trump continued to make his position clear that the nation needed: College Football! With fans in the stands!!

In unrelated news, Elon Musk unveiled a pig with a computer chip in its brain

Media sedative Joe Biden selected Kamala Harris as his running mate. The GOP was poised to re-nominate **Trump, the Law-and-Order President**!

– CRIMINAL INDICTMENTS BY ADMINISTRATION –

Obama – 0	Ford – 1 Carter – 1		George H.W. Bush - 1
Clinton – 2	George W. Bush – 16	Reagan – 26	Nixon – 76

Donald J. Trump - *215*

Kellyanne Conway announced that she was resigning from her post as Trumpenstein's Senior Adviser of Alternate Facts. The announcement came just hours after one of Mrs. Conway's daughters tweeted that her mother's job had "*ruined* [her] *life*" and wanted "*emancipation*."

Trump Facts – in a NY Times interview on his plans for four more years in office: "*But so I think, I think it would be, I think it would be very, very, I think we'd have a very, very solid, we would continue what we're doing, we'd solidify what we've done, and we have other things on our plate that we want to get done.*"

RNC Platform (summarized)... Up is Down. **DNC Platform** (summarized)... Left is Right

August:
At the approach
of
Evening storms, dragonflies
Zigzag toward Queen Anne's Lace
Piggy-backing a ride on a comfortless
breeze –
Backstitching – toward the ceaseless

Psychotic buzzing of a rhythmless
Cicada squabble, under halos
Of celestial spheres and
Distant, red-light
Emissions

———

Timing the thunder
In a long month of long days
Signs of confused thinking interleave
With reality, lost to the bones of a narrative
Entombed in the somber granite of Lacan's idea

———

The goal of psychoanalysis is not to get cured
but to confront the human condition

Sometimes referred to as "the French Freud," Jacques Marie Émile Lacan
was a French psychoanalyst and psychiatrist.

FAMILY MATTERS

Last we heard from him
was a phone call on a Tuesday night
right in the middle of dinner.   Dad got up
answered   and when he came back minutes later
all he said was, "It was Eddie. He's going to Las Vegas.
Doesn't expect he'll see us again. Wanted to say good-bye."
Dinner continued in silence.   It was just a few years later
again during dinner, that Dad got a collect call from a man
in Detroit who said he'd found our phone number – in
Eddie's wallet : *he was the baby of the family* : *nobody*
thought he'd be the first one to die. Hard to believe
it's been twenty years now –

C'mon dad, answer the phone.

KODAK MOMENTS

In Detroit, back when the family

Get-togethers were recorded with an

Instamatic, mom took her rolls of film to

Cunningham's or Kinsel Drugs for developing

A week later she'd pick up her glossy B&W prints

Then put them in the albums I'm now leafing through

And I'm finding her way of framing subjects kind

Of comical when viewed through the context of years ...

Naturally, there were lots of mom & dad pictures – *more often than not*

with a pitcher of margaritas – but there was also a select group that soundlessly

Seemed to say: - UGH [!] , you'll pay for this.

                    - Can't believe you wore that.

                    - OMG! *What* were you *thinking!?!*

Which in turn served as artful companion pieces to

Mom's trio of recurring themes:

                    - People posing on driveways.

                    - Shirtless photos of my father.

                    - Women with *really* bad hair.

Except for the dried remains of a long-legged dead spider, the albums had been

Untouched – boxed and stored in the garage for a year – and I'm pretty sure

She knew (she *must* have known) her albums would one day be laugh-out-loud

Funny to see. The images are changeless, like key syllables in charades, and of a

Silent vocabulary that seemed to say: *Life? It's confusing. Tequila was a godsend.*

TWENTY QUESTIONS

Just before Gertrude Stein died, she was able to ask, *"What is the answer?"*
Receiving no response, her last words were... *"In that case, what is the question?"*

[... III ...]

Attending a funeral awaiting Amen
brings to mind Keats's plea, but
mid-thought I stop
to consider Coronis in a decorative corbel
envision the tattletale, and ever so briefly
riddle the following question:
If *I* were a clever crow
would I have pecked Ischys's eyes?

[.. II ..]

What do you require?

Flagellants - they need to bleed.

What is superfluous?

Work, money, life, and death.

What is essential?

Slavic detachment.

What is the purpose of life?

*To name the things we destroy
and forgive ourselves with song.*

Are there more than two truths in life?

*Death is surely one; do you doubt that
doubt could be the only other?*

What is infallible dogma?

Everything is for sale.

[. I .]

In moments of powerlessness and uncertainty

What is the difference between a boxcar and a meat locker?

How are the subject and subjected different?

When is morality not situational?

The amygdala jump starts the brain into analytical overdrive

If you're not concerned by social unrest how are you not part of the problem?

What if the mark of Cain was simply what we now call Caucasian?

Can you state with any certainty this is not a simulation?

In the casual solitude of an oxygen machine

By definition, at what point do s*mall* wars stop being small?

Why are there *permissible* levels of radiation?

When is *enough* ENOUGH?

Fire is the rapid acquisition of oxygen

[.]

Days before my mother dies – speaking in her croaky little voice

filled with mischief, she sez – *Pull my finger.* I say – *What?*

Rolling her eyes, she smiles an impish smile, and I go – *OMG!*

MOM MODE

emerged when an unsympathetic
jungle paused at the bloated river's bend
to meet & greet the breathless gathering – (*we*
fished 'em out & swaddled the departed in body bags)

      Raging

          weeds and civilization
          had long since run out of things to say to me

          Anonymity filled the trees
          the trails, the expectancies
              like the dead hour
              in a kill zone –
          words still do not come easily

          There is little solace
          to be found in who I am now
          or that was way back when ...
          I spoke with no one
              and
          no one spoke for me

The smell and ambiguity of drifting sands are the same
Possessed of the knowledge of pitch and rhythm, there is
little doubt that the depth – the purpose of horizontal dialog
is to unite darkness and bramble – provide structure and shape
to unexceptional futures – and to frame the manner in which this
                  will come to be defined at the periphery

But even these insights do not fully prepare you
for making decisions about your mother's morphine drip
and her life support – because there are no life-signs –
and because your father has asked you to make these decisions –
because he says he can't ... and you understand

CREMAINS

The body in decline is startling to see …

Mandelbrot-like patterns of Before and

After in the open storehouse of our emotions.

Navigating beauty & pain

We absorb the difference

Between illness & disease

Between will & intent, between

Falsehoods, to contemplate certain

Truths – like the jarring realization that, depending

On the size of an individual, the ignition temperature

Essential to incinerating a body – to reduce it to ash –

Is about the same as the heat range used to glaze raku.

Interfused with the etymology of cremains (*first used in 1947*)

Is the search result that revealed cremains are not ashes

After all, but 8 or 9 pounds of pulverized bone.

   (*about the weight of a child's bowling ball*)

Meaningless mile-a-minute mind's-eye vignettes were on

Endless replay at the end. I'm still trying to make sense of

Your way of looking at things. Like, what were you really

Trying to tell me when you pulled me close and whispered

–The lifespan of some parrots can be upwards of 100 years–

MR DUBITO WRITES A DEATH POEM

Reading about Bashō emboldens Mr Dubito to muse
– How best to sum up what I have learned about life –
When nothing comes to mind, he chuckles ...

:: *the anagram of listen is silent* ::

Like Bashō, he's opposed to the belief ~

the purpose of one's life journey
is to compose a death poem

Nevertheless, to honor Bashō, Mr Dubito writes:

. . .

the sum of a brash

seamless unity   dimpled

with eerie frissons

. . .

Mr Dubito sez ...

The Gates of the Mind
are predisposed, open
to even the slightest
particle of experience

OBSERVATIONS

In The Theory and Practice of Rivers, Jim Harrison writes

"... *it is nearly impossible to surprise ourselves.*"

But *I am* surprised/glancing at my wrist/checking the time

– feels so strange –

I haven't

Worn a watch in ten years ... Is there a

Name for the above-mentioned

Mis-connect – the synapse that

Misfired – or was it otherworldly

A one-time-only window that opened

A different version of your subconscious:

The mental puree of *alternate* Here & Now's

Being unexpectedly stimulated in a

Way that puts you in mind of a possible

Future/Past that may come to pass in a Zen

Garden where, bowing before a meditating monk

You remove your watch/place it at his feet: it will feel

Like a metaphor for mindful meditation – a figurative point

Of reference – notwithstanding

How can it be almost September –

Spring Primrose are still in bloom

Dusk: three egrets enact a theatrical dance in a small lily pond

Two face northeast, one southwest – when a fourth joins them

You enter a story where every day ends like this & life is perfect

(9) – THE FUTURE'S COMING AND THERE'S NO PLACE TO HIDE

While discussing the shooting of Jacob Blake with Fox News' Laura Ingraham, Lawnorder said sometimes an officer *"makes a mistake"* or *"chokes"* under pressure, *"Just like in a golf tournament, they miss a three-foot putt."*

[NOTE: Police shot Blake in the back – 7 times. That's nothing like a missed 3-foot putt.]

Two deputies from the Los Angeles County Sheriff's Department shot [15 times] and killed Dijon Kizzee, a 29-year old Black man, on a sunny Monday afternoon, after he dropped his bike and ran when they attempted to stop him for *"riding a bicycle in an unlawful manner."*

Lost in translation: An autistic 13-year-old boy in Glendale, Utah, was shot – several times – by police officers after his mother called 911 for help with his mental health crisis and told the 911 operator that her son needed to be taken to hospital for treatment.

A special prosecutor announced that a Missouri police officer who claimed a woman was preparing to shoot him during a traffic stop over the summer would not be charged for fatally shooting the woman. Police did not find a gun in the car and her family and friends said she did not own one.

Portland Police made multiple arrests as the Oregon city neared 100 days of demonstrations against racism and police brutality, which at times had turned violent.

Police had given more than 100 people head injuries with so-called less-lethal ammunition such as rubber bullets at protests this summer, according to the group Physicians for Human Rights (PHR).

A U.S. District Court judge partially granted a restraining order preventing Detroit police from responding to peaceful demonstrations with *"beatings, tear gas, pepper spray, rubber bullets, sound cannons, flash grenades, chokeholds, and mass arrests."*

Viewer impressions of the U.S. Presidential Debate: *No strategy, just kill and eat :: This was not a debate in any meaningful sense :: A mess :: A dumpster fire on steroids :: An hour and a half of insults :: Undignified :: Unpresidential :: Chaotic :: Childish :: Grueling :: A national humiliation :: A TV duel like a car accident :: A total disaster ...*

– Biden raised nearly $4 million in one hour after the shit show –

The Hair Apparent refused to commit to a peaceful transfer of power if he were to lose in November's election, saying he believed the election result could end up in the U.S. Supreme Court, as he cast doubt on postal voting. *"I've been complaining very strongly about the ballots, and the ballots are a disaster."*

BULLETPROOF: bag o' tricks

Backpacks ... plus colorful artwork meant to engage children. Comes with
                'levels of protection' ranging from pistols to AR-15 style rifles!

Backpack Inserts ... Don't want to pop for a full-blown *backpack* just yet? Got
                ya' covered with a 'Tank the Turtle' *insert*, a kindergarten-
                friendly ballistic shield mascot – *Kids, use your shells!* ☺

Blast Mitigation Window Film ... a micro-layered laminate designed to prevent
                glass from shattering [!] when struck by
                bullets from a *semi*-automatic rifle. Wow!

Classroom Desks ... Yeah, thass what I'm talkin' 'bout: Deployable Ballistics!

Clipboards ...not just any BULLETPROOF clipboard, either. These are *decorated* [!]
                For teachers!! Choose from: Palm-Frond! Pink Sunset! & Starry Night!

Collapsible Safe Rooms ... You're thinkin', clipboard/ schmipboard – for $60K
                everyone *in this rapid-access classroom* is
                ~~BULLETPROOF~~ uh, protected. Wait ... what?

Hand-Held Shield ... has 'ACTIVE SHOOTER PROTECTION' printed right on it!
                So *helpful* in a full-blown panic situation w/guns! Kids (sigh).

Hoodies ... gotta' have 'em. BULLETPROOF hoodies! Finally! But wait, there's more
... been shot wearing a BULLETPROOF hoodie? No worries – FREE OF CHARGE –
replacements are available. Just send a copy of the police report or a news clip.

Pencil Pouches ... they're just like a regular pencil pouch – but w/*super powers!*

Portable-Dry-Erase-Board ... made of Ballistic! Armor! Plates! Another must-
                have for schools! And it *'blends in'*.

Three-Ring Binders ... looking for something more covert? Designed to hang
                from a child's neck – with a hidden strap – you'll
                immediately wish it came in pink.

                                    * * *

        – There have been over 230 school shootings in the US in the past ten years –

There is no evidence that any of the 'target-hardening' measures listed make schools safer

Pythagoras proved that musical tonality

is based on mathematical relationships, but

Pythagoras was wrong about integer ratios

making a chord sound beautiful   We

prefer slight amounts of deviation

*

The final movement

from

Mozart's Requiem in D minor

is titled *LACRIMOSA*

(from the Latin, for "*weeping/tearful*")

music   about facing mortality

that Mozart wrote on his deathbed ...

*

and perhaps *weeping/tearful* is also a wish

– based on mathematical imperfections –

for a different set of circumstances

that

would have clearly indicated

that that

was not a gun

EDICT OF GRACE: in which decrees from the Spanish Inquisition are repurposed
[Texas Senate Bill 8!]

After ~~mass~~ *your arrest* ~~Dominican Inquisitors~~ *Prosecutors* will ~~discuss~~ *mansplain* ~~heresy and~~ why you can't ~~xxxxxxxxx~~ *have an abortion*. (Your body, my choice.)

The goal of ~~an Inquisitor~~ *a Prosecutor* is to extract a confession.
(The goal of Senate Bill 8 is to inform: *you know, you really are fucked*.)

Use of torture to extract confessions is no longer sanctioned ~~by the church~~.
(However, bounty-hunters *can* stalk those who *"aid & abet"*. [$10k!])

The accused does not have the right to counsel and must testify against herself.
(The accuser must also testify!)

The accused may not confront the accuser.
(Well, *duh!* What would be the point of that?)

An accuser may be a family member, friend, neighbor, UBER/LYFT driver, stranger, or known criminal ...

and

here

come

PAIN and

DESPAIR!

Ambassadors

of the lonely place

: You've heard them :

harmonizing hauntingly

barren parodies of life like

!! ~~*EL EDICTO DE GRACIA*~~ !!

the *"HEARTBEAT BILL"* – stalkers

endlessly detailing again & again

convoluted tales of complicity and

your subsequent points of departure

AFTER THE VIVISEPULTURE

Can you picture a woman in Nigeria

    Can you picture her buried

Alive, in the ground, up to her neck

    Now, imagine an obscenity

That would make you want to stone her

    I will tell you what has happened ...

    Can you picture a woman in Nigeria

        Charged with adultery, she defends herself

    The sentence is: *GUILTY!!* She will be stoned to death

        By the people of the village where she lives

    She has a name ...

        Can you picture a woman named Safiya

    Can you picture a baby

        Not yet weaned

    That serves as evidence of the act

        Which now calls for the death of her mother

    It is written, so they say

I wonder

    How a divorced woman living alone can commit adultery

Ahhh, but they point to the baby – Wait, you say

    What about the man

Ahhh, it was not a consideration

    You see, he confessed to nothing

And the act was not witnessed

    By four members (in good standing)

Of his faith ...

        But I digress

      After Safiya's been buried   alive

        In the ground to her neck

    The village will be invited to gather

        Stones and throw them at her head

And throw   and throw

        And throw and throw and throw

And as they throw, they'll create & fashion

        Her sanguinary shroud of stone

You may wonder

    What will happen to the baby

Who will tell her of her mother

    Will she ask

        Did

      You throw a stone

      Was it the first

      Were you

      Without

      Sin

THE KULESHOV EFFECT

At the independent bookstore checkout

the associate inquires —

Are you the kind of reader ...

The customer interrupts/sez

Maybe/blinking ensues/eye

contact is re-established, and

the associate now asks, *Are you*

the type of person who judges a

book by its cover? [the book cover in

question is a stylized drawing of a psycho

red rooster dodging smok'n-hot shell-casings]

No, that would not be possible for this book; this

is a story about a kidnapping in the Philippines that

involves a meth-addled cab driver — and his feathered

friend — the customer points out as he waits for a receipt

*

It turns out the associate's cousin — *has been*

living in the Philippines these past three

years with his 12-year-old son ...

[in rapid succession the following come to mind]

-   MacArthur — "I Shall Return!"
-   the in-law who served in the Peace Corps
-   salting a Filipino's farmland
-   the foreign service job offer that never materialized
-   the certifiable insanity that was Rodrigo Duterte

... looking up he sez, *That must be challenging*

then turns and heads for the door to the parking lot

*

To the casual observer, this quiet man

might appear pleasant & unassuming

He remembers killing men, remem

-bers and remembers and *knows*

no amount of alcohol, drugs

love, religion, meditation

  or salt   can make that

go away – he thinks

Eastwood got it right

in 'Unforgiven', *it's*

a helluva thing

killin' a man ...

. . .

In the Philippines

typhoons and heavy downpours begin to tail off in mid-to-late October.

But it can go either way –

floods, mudslides, and typhoons are regular occurrences, as well.

(10) – THE WORLD HAS ALWAYS BEEN A MESSY PLACE

Department of CMTSU: During a speech at the 75th annual Al Smith Dinner at the White House, Trump declared: *"the end of the pandemic is in sight"*. Later he announced (via tweet) that both he and Malaria had tested positive for COVID-19. Tweets for Trump were split between *"thoughts and prayers"* and *"told you so."*

MEANWHILE: the privately-owned White House Gift Shop marked the release of its newest commemorative: For $100, you could pre-order a coin, with a *"design suggestive of superhero graphic art,"* that declared:

> "President Donald J. Trump Defeats COVID."

A fly generated the most buzz from the VP Debate. For approximately two minutes, a fly landed on Vice-President Mike Pence's head. The fly seemed to unite people on both sides of the aisle with most agreeing it was probably the most memorable thing that happened that night, which was so ironic – the debate itself was like flies on shit. Recapping the VP Debate: Pence repeatedly interrupted Sen. Kamala Harris, ignored the moderator, went over time, and refused to directly answer the questions.

WHAT IF I TOLD YOU THIS WAS THE TRUMP CAMPAIGN CHECKLIST FOR REELECTION

Basic civility in public discourse ... butchered ✓

Worst race relations in half a century ... *"shoot 'em"*

Obstruct voter registration and online voting ... ongoing

Rampant, unchecked lying about almost everything ... done ✓

Denigration of relations with other countries & alliances ... pick one

Worst economic collapse since the Great Depression ... 56M out of work

Nakedly succoring white supremacists and right-wing terrorists ...*"stand-by"* ✓

America's reputation as a reliable leader of the international community ... erased

~~person.woman.man.camera.tv~~   division.discord.chaos.vitriol.hate

MEANWHILE: Caroline Giuliani, daughter of former NYC mayor Rudy Giuliani – Trump's personal attorney – urged Americans to *"end this nightmare"* by voting for Democratic nominees Biden & Harris.

DREAM 1

In the recurring dream
a woman sits herself down
-hill from a huckleberry bush ...
picking uphill allows her to see
cloaked clusters of low berries
among simple oblong leaves

Q. What will you do with the berries?
A. I wish to speak to the Great Spirit.

DREAM 2

We were in a place of lapis fields and sky
Then we ate stones in Shadowland
Both views are inexpressible

DREAM ∞

This is the dream that is inexhaustible

_____

This first dream speaks of humble perseverance.
The second alludes to the Indian Removal Act of 1830.
The final dream is very much about endless white man lies.

SAVAGES

I. What we were taught ...

Out of fear we turned to the anarchy of confession & scorpion-like prescriptions

Nostalgia was not explored: there would be no merging of past & present

Radiant fictions helped to distract us from uncertain futures

Necessity would blur risk and failure chronologically

II. What was learned ...

Questionable behaviors in response to stress are symbolic attempts at flight

This is the no-man's land of dizzy spells and life-threatening symptoms

Silently we know you have lied to us in ways we barely comprehend

We would never learn the right time and way to do or say things

III. What was unearthed ...

The past changed before our
                eyes obsidian and obscene
not the way light escapes the departed
                nor the way sand enters a wound but
traveling mad curvilinear distances as if searching
                for a prescription on the reverse side of an old
mirror with the stubborn insistence of a truncated limb ...
                Imaginative confessions suggest that sex in cinema
the voyeuristic intimacy the expressive caresses the undulate
                filling of orifices corrupted the priesthood Coming
from the world of *il castrato* I suppose that makes some
                sort of sense but it doesn't begin to explain
hundreds of unmarked schoolyard graves at the
                sites of former Canadian residential
schools for Indigenous children Does it

***

From the 19th century until the 1970s, more than 150,000 Indigenous children were forced to attend state-funded Christian schools, the majority of them run by Roman Catholic missionary congregations, in a campaign to assimilate them into Canadian society. The Canadian government has admitted that physical *and* sexual abuse was rampant in the schools, with students beaten for speaking their native languages.

* * *

On October 25, 2024, a Presidential Joe Biden formally apologized to Native Americans for what he described as "one of the most horrific chapters in American history," government-funded boarding schools that abused indigenous children and forced them to assimilate over a 150-year period. At least 18,000 children were taken from their families and forced to attend more than 400 boarding schools across 37 states or then-territories between 1819 and 1969. At least 973 Native American children died while attending these federal boarding schools.

THE UNEXPECTED POETRY OF STALIN'S JOURNAL
[The Tehran Conference: 28 November – 1 December, 1943]

[28 November]

Roosevelt and Churchill
          they are like lullabies
of contemporary myth: I can *feel*
          over-laurelled surrealism: I *hear*
patriotic songs entrenched in their skeptical sighs
          Disoriented, their vacillations are *vhispering*:
Yes! Let's make harmony with Joseph Vissarionovich!

[29 November]

My moody   ironic   guilt-free emotions
          are superbly camouflaged: I appear
                    beguiling
like The Stalinist Spring of Reluctant Courtesans
          or the prelude to an execution ...

[30 November]

... Secretly, I entertain the articulation of mystic rapture –
In Lubyanka, persona non grata will dance for the Cheka!

[1 December]

:: I foresee Russia's future ::

I sit high and see far
          Shrewd and wise
                    In an age of clever

                    Our narrative remains
          Arcane, but more expressive
Like burn marks on the horizon

Code-named Eureka, the Tehran Conference was the first of two wartime meetings held during WWII that were attended by the key allied leaders Stalin, Churchill, and Roosevelt. The main objective of the United States and Great Britain was to ensure full cooperation and assistance from the Soviet Union for their war policies. Stalin agreed, but at a price: Roosevelt and Churchill would have to support his reign and the partisans in Yugoslavia, and also allow for the manipulation of the border between Poland and the USSR. Churchill and Roosevelt also consented to the USSR setting up puppet communist governments in Poland, Czechoslovakia, the Baltic states, Romania, and other Eastern European countries which would result in a loss of freedom by these countries for the next fifty years and would be the genesis of the Cold War.

I sit high and see far – Russian proverb

I knew something had changed
he said, *the night the colonel said –*

Shoot anything that moves!

[memories begin staking claims]

During the Second World War, after the Battle of the Bulge, my
father's Armored Unit approached a farm in Bastogne [*bonjour!*] and
asked, *Would the farmer and his wife be agreeable to having the
Americans make camp on their farm.* By way of reply the couple
began to cry, and after hugging each of the men, motioned for them to
follow. The old man led them into a barn, and after revealing then
disappearing thru a hidden trap door, re-emerged with dozens of fresh
eggs and several bottles of Cognac that he'd hidden from the Germans
who had previously occupied his home. Then they all drank and ate
scrambled eggs ...

It happened so long ago, he said
it's like it was all a movie

—

Creased and torn black & white photos
Stained glass windows
A remote Christian childhood
Emotion-stained syllables
Fixed-narratives of change
It was the time of the blood moon –
Our histories are increasingly incomprehensible

—

Inseparable
my parents were married for 65 years – a
sudden cancer took my mother – her urn is
still dallying on their dining room table

During the days now, dad, he mostly
dozes   Evenings are devoted to
watching classic movies on TV

—

And yes, it does sometimes feel like
we're all in some kind of movie, I mean I
sure never thought we'd be sitting here
drifting toward the edge of longish days
having this kind of conversation ...

Dad said –

You

know

at times

my life felt full

of the concept of duende

Now it just feels like THE END

in a meandering anamorphic movie

Without thinking, I blurt – anamorphic?

Closing his eyes, Dad sez – CinemaScope –

Horizontal compression of the image during filming

(11) — WHAT'S ORANGE ON THE OUTSIDE,

hollow on the inside, and needs

to be thrown out in November?

Each year, lexicographers at Oxford Languages, the maker of the Oxford English Dictionary, choose a single word or phrase to define the past 12 months. In 2018, it was "toxic." In 2019, it was "climate emergency." For 2020 they couldn't choose a 'single' one. Instead, they chose a bunch... Juneteenth, Black Lives Matter, systemic racism, coronavirus, COVID-19, pandemic, superspreader, lockdown, self-quarantine, community transmission, shelter-in-place, stay-at-home, self-isolate, covidiots, Blursday, social distancing, mask-shaming, flattening the curve, and reopening.

Department of: This is Why You Need to VOTE: Trump told associates he intended to declare premature victory on Election Night so as to cast doubt on the integrity of the election and undermine the validity of uncounted mail-in ballots in the days after.

Blasting the former-vice-president for spreading misinformation at this perilous time for democracy, media figures across the political spectrum condemned Joe Biden for his baseless claim that the nation would come together once the election was over.

— ELECTION DAY IN AMERICA — After a tumultuous four years Americans headed to the polls to choose whether to stay the course with Trump, or elect Joe Biden as their next president.

— ELECTION DAY+4 IN AMERICA — And on Saturday it happened: Biden/ Harris declared winner!

MEANWHILE: Trump was considering pardoning himself, and briefly participated in the opening comments of the virtual G-20 summit "Pandemic Preparedness and Response" then skipped the rest of the conference to play golf.

MEANWHILE: Beijing passed a resolution allowing Hong Kong's city government to dismiss politicians deemed a threat to national security and disqualified 4 members.

[Q. How many fingers am I holding up?   A. How many do you want there to be?]

MEANWHILE: The U.S. was joined by the UK in declining to participate in an international treaty aimed at stopping plastics from flowing into the world's oceans and other natural habitats. MEANWHILE: *Pepsi unveiled its first 2-liter bottle redesign in nearly 30 years!* The new plastic bottle has an enhanced "*grip point*" at the bottom that's 25% slimmer than the old plastic bottle, making the "*modern, functional and easy-to-use bottle*" easier to pour!

DREAM INTERPRETATION: in which Samuel L. Jackson (appearing as – [S~L. J])
makes clear this poem's many hidden meanings

November in Mexico – the arrival of *Día de los Muertos.*

Monarch butterflies draw near with the spirits of the departed.

– [S~L. J] ... *In Mexico, 98% of murders remain unresolved ...*

History is nothing more than sanitized statistics about past events

and the maladroit people who thought they could master any subtlety.

– [S~L. J] ... *Fools and motherfuckers rule the world ...*

An old man crosses the street – a fleeting custodian of solace, a verb

in certain circumstances.

– [S~L. J] ... *Like Levertov said, "The poet must never lose despair"...*

A woman says she can't be arrested in the middle of the night – cuz she's White.

Meanwhile, several Walmart employees fatally crush a Black shoplifter.

– [S~L. J] ... *Everything is a matter of perception ...*

To feel like a breathless monk in an espresso bar is to be desperate.

To be desperate may simply be a side effect.

– [S~L. J] ... *Never underestimate the difference between a motherfucker*

and a large group of motherfuckers ...

Kneeling, reading haiku in Japanese - one vertical line/not three horizontals.

The line reinforces the quality of being transient despite its daunting length.

– [S~L. J] ... *Bee-cuz, the opposite of a Zen motherfucker's truth is also true ...*

TEMPTATION

The complex relationship with abstraction –

that it was so meticulously produced!

You couldn't help but question

the seductive moth-like speculations

those overwhelmingly idealized distortions

gasping for relevance like guttering red candles

[Q.] Are we drawn to the light

the dark

or the contrast

[A.] Their plural presence ...

the array is a still life: brief sightlines

of New York in November acquiescing

to Fire and Ice, embracing their shadows –

in the way a Chinese gateway might

linger in the moonlit shimmer

of a still point on a polished human skull –

exploring flights of fancy

and the geography of what we cannot resist

DREAM INTERPRETATION: wherein a footnote reminds us of Gogol's dreams

the mutinous inner voices full of abnegation and scorn

the farcical fascination and flirtation with madness

the artistic perversity, the metaphysical shudder

the fermenting congruity of clarity & cruelty

the lazy prejudices, the festering phrases

the duplicitous blue corpse, left

face down in its coffin

———————

Yes, Nikolai, these dreams are the work of the devil!
They tell you to burn your manuscripts!!

* * *

Mark Meadows, White House Chief of Staff under the Trump administration, was said to have routinely burned documents in his White House office fireplace following official meetings.

Last life, present life, next life – one

    plus one plus one still makes one.

There was no attempt to restrain him from tweeting on Twitter

    gaslighting that incurable division between life and theater.

Things that were supposedly – but not necessarily – true or real

    became a series of nonsensical explanations.

And if you missed the season-ending episode ...

    [SPOILER ALERT]

the setting was somber, as if the small hours of night were lost

    in introspection. The self-centered orange dog was

lying, untroubled, curled up like a donut ... putting one in mind of

    an ouroboros delightedly devouring its own tail.

(12) – EOY WRAP UP

– President-elect Biden and VP Harris – Time magazine's Person of the Year! –

Trump released a 46-minute video [rant] denouncing the election as *"rigged"* [not] while repeating his baseless allegations of voter fraud that he claimed was *"massive"* [not] and *"on a scale never seen before"* [as in non-existent? Then yes.].

WHAT IF I TOLD YOU THE ABILITY TO SPEAK DOES NOT MAKE YOU INTELLIGENT

The Arecibo radio telescope in Puerto Rico *collapsed*, but the SpaceX launch of the new unmanned Starship prototype rocket soared to record-setting heights. CEO Elon Musk called the mission a success despite the ship *exploding*. On impact. As it landed.

Murder was up 36 percent throughout the year compared to the same period in 2019. (Over 1,436,000 people have been killed by guns in the US since John Lennon was shot and killed as he entered the Dakota apartment building in New York 12/8/1980.)

Deaths of Afghan civilians in air raids carried out by the US and its allies *"increased dramatically"* since 2017 when Washington loosened its criteria and escalated attacks on the Taliban. After more than a *TRILLION fucking* dollars spent, General Mark Milley, Chairman of the Joint Chiefs of Staff, said that the US had *"achieved a modicum of success"* in Afghanistan. WTF!! A *modicum* of success? *Are you fucking kidding me!?!*

Thai protesters demonstrated in Bangkok to demand more action to help seafood sellers hit by a COVID-19 outbreak where 1,500 infections were linked to a shrimp market outside Bangkok. The government urged people to eat more shellfish.

New record-high COVID-19 hospitalizations were reported in the US and passed 100,000 for the first time, a figure that doubled since early November.

France mobilized 100,000 police to break up New Year's Eve parties and enforce a COVID night-time curfew. Many cities simply cancelled events. In America we were treated to watching Anderson Cooper do shots of tequila.

Dutch prosecutors said Trump's Twitter account was hacked by someone guessing his password: MAGA2020! Pundits promptly provided a smorgasbord of suggested passwords, among them – *ShutTheFuckUp2020!,* and *person-woman-man-camera-tv!*

Trump signed an executive order requiring *"beautiful"* architecture as the preferred style for federal buildings, but millions of Americans saw their jobless benefits expire when he refused to sign into law a $2.3 trillion pandemic aid and spending package saying it did not do enough to help everyday people.

WHAT IF I TOLD YOU "1984" WAS NOT AN INSTRUCTION MANUAL

WHEN THOSE CURSÉD ENTER FLAMES

"The past is a foreign country: they do things differently there"
L. P. Hartley

When those curséd enter flames

the speed of adjustment naturally quickens.

Decomposing in degrees of madness

nerves burn while sensations flee

the tortured torso's abandoned

boundary and inharmonious

soul.

There once was little doubt that

where companion angels might show

polite concern, the Devil feared a miraculous

preaching severed-head held by a martyred cephalophore.

Confessions beyond comprehension may

echo the past, but the past

is not a foreign land ...

it's a suicide note.

(13) – LIKE SIMPLE PLOT TWISTS

Snowfall in Madrid was reportedly the heaviest in at least 40 years. MEANWHILE: A Boeing 737 passenger plane carrying 62 people was believed to have crashed into the sea shortly after take-off from Indonesia's capital Jakarta. MEANWHILE: Chinese authorities told residents in two cities south of Beijing to stay home for seven days as they tried to stamp out a new COVID-19 outbreak. MEANWHILE: Iran's elite Islamic Revolutionary Guard Corps [IRGC] unveiled a huge underground missile base along the Persian Gulf coast amid heightened tensions with the United States. MEANWHILE: Nearly *50,000* people were evacuated in Malaysia after monsoon rains pounded the country's east coast causing what residents described as the worst flooding in half a century. MEANWHILE: A *"MAJOR INCIDENT"* was declared in London, with warnings hospitals in the UK capital could be overwhelmed with coronavirus patients if people did not stay at home. MEANWHILE: U.S. leaders largely remained silent on the pandemic in the aftermath of the ~~attempted insurrection riot~~ JAN6 rally. MEANWHILE: The COVID Tracking Project recorded approximately 3,777 US coronavirus-related deaths in one day alone. MEANWHILE: the Lord of Lies told aides he thought it might be a *really* good idea to pre-emptively pardon himself!

> The repeated percussions were like
> lifeless promises, thin tissues of
> truths we believed in
>
> We were hard-pressed to recognize
> wisdom can change in the same way
> derelict structures devoid of people
> become their own songs, journeys
> entwined with dissimilar things
> a gradual decay, a betrayal of
> form that occurs at a certain
> age What did not change
> was the sum of our
> decisions
>
> There are no concessions in a frame within a frame
> A place can have many lives and meanings
>
> [our lies to ourselves were so beautiful]

ON THE SIXTH DAY

"Be there, will be wild!"

And so it came to pass –
they wallowed in capricious depths
changing fact to alter outcome
armored in warm delusional permutations
of pantomime and sly innuendo ...
disciples of the false prophet.

"I was slipping in people's blood."

This is what remains, these are the unfinished parts.

< YOU SAID >

– A whole world looks to see what we will do –

– it was Change We Can Believe In –

– Compassionate Conservatism was your approach –

– all the right words : to get the country moving again –

: to get the hostages – I remember :

– *Read My Lips* –

< YOU EXPLAINED >

: Peace and Honor :

: A Great Society : We Shall

Overcome : That You Would Be

GRANTING a PARDON to : *I am not a crook*

< YUP, Y'ALL GAVE US >

WATERGATE   JAN6   the Bay of Pigs

Iran-Contra   Bank Bailouts   *the Cold War*

SANCTIONS!   Kissinger   the DOMINO Theory

Vietnam   Korea   'made-up' stories of WMD's

RECESSIONS INSURRECTIONISTS! Afghanistan

targeted killings using MISSILES & DRONES

the Collapse of the American Dream – and

every four years, in years divisible by four

unfailingly you're like a broken thermostat

sending a false sense of hope and the same

empty rhetoric how things will get better and

like *magic,* we believe: WHAT is *WRONG with us!?!*

(Subjective Narrative)

Collectively we paused
Paid our respects

Throughout the word temple
hollow lamentations echoed
the ceaseless candor of the dead

"Thoughts and prayers!"

COLLATERAL: /kə-lăt'ər-əl/   [adjective]

   - Situated or running side by side; parallel.

   - Coinciding in tendency or effect; concomitant or accompanying.

   – *"Everything we do is a fiction until it's a fact."* –

1.   On average, police in the United States shoot and kill more than 1,000
         people every year, according to an ongoing analysis by The Washington Post.

The *former* president, declaring his candidacy for the 2024 Presidential Election, said he wanted to *expand* the use of the death penalty, and bring back death by firing squad, by hanging, and by guillotine [!], if re-elected. He also suggested *televising* footage of executions … he would later pile on his crime & punishment stance, saying – if police were allowed *"one real rough, nasty"* and *"violent day"* crime would be eliminated – *"immediately."*

DAMAGE: / 'da-mij/   [verb]

   - (transitive) to cause damage to

   - (intransitive) to suffer damage

   – You've no idea what's beyond the door that you're trying to open –

2.   And BTW, this is not how we should be raising our children …

Picture where you live: a hop, skip, and a jump away, 95% of schools conduct drills for a shooting and/or employ other means of protection – metal detectors, armed guards, locked doors, arming teachers. Today in America, the number one killer of children is guns. Once America decided this was bearable, the gun debate in all but name was over …

   – FUCK YOUR THOUGHTS AND PRAYERS –

FLASHBULB MEMORIES [& marginalia]

Bagging my groceries, the associate sez, So do you

have plans for the day? And I must admit things

did not go according to plan after I said yes

      Grace & Virtue/Fate vs Chance ...

            – sometimes it's the way the paint chips –

      Early August – on the patio with a proper

      -ly chilled French Rose – and apolitical crickets

            : September :

            A Wedding [!]

            Batman Day &

            the Fall Equinox

            So much to celebr8!

You're 8 years old, sitting alone in the dark –

on gramma's living room sofa – watching

Hockey Night in Canada on a black & white TV

      You hear *clinking* in the kitchen: bottles

of Cincinnati Cream – a lager from Canada – are opened

beer is poured/pinochle cards : *ritualistically shuffled*/you try

to make sense of adulting/to this day you hate hockey and card games

      The male carpenter bee, having no stinger

      has limited responses to human threats

To be filled with wow by a poem can be like

      introducing a 3-yr-old to a kaleidoscope

of cosmos, nasturtiums, and zinnias in full bloom ...

      whereas with happy-go-lucky milkweed

reactions can go either way

      The windows and doors are still open although

        evening temperatures tend to drop

        precipitously this time of year

      – lightning is marbling the night sky –

      Once you've fallen down a few stairs you realize

      getting old is more than just a tiresome punchline

For similar reasons, thoughtful deployment of a back scratcher

in a hard to reach place can feel like the height of pleasure ...

Start a list – how we fucked it all up *: Kissinger : Enron : the Shah of Iran*

      : Citizens United : televangelists : semi-automatic weapons

      : J. Edgar Hoover : McCarthyism : Strom Thurmond

  : Lobbyists : Gingrich : Lehman Brothers : Rumsfeld : Reality TV ...

         *

      Chernobyl in English means 'wormwood'.

      Wormwood is the name of the great star that

      fell from the heavens in the Book of Revelations

FRAGMENTS

Memories beyond comprehension reside in each of us.

        Visions of the life that could have been.

Ambassadors of the lonely place.

Age will do this. Inky accumulations

        linger in your pivots and slurs

like vain repetitions of prayer.

You realize that everyday issues

        of things not said or written are like truth

and fact to the wind. To be desperate may simply be a side effect

of the unfinished parts – like

        attending a funeral awaiting amen. That kind of conversation.

There's no playbook for this.

Plagued with doubt you will be reminded

        of attempts to be content that did not serve you.

Not for the first time, binary numbers appear

to represent the sum of family interruptions and resentful

        eyes of children. To reorient yourself with life's purpose

and meaning, plant your feet firmly & take hold of your unpeaceful head ...

        repeat after me: There is a balm in Gilead ...

           "There is a bomb in Gilead"

[2020 HINDSIGHT – January – THIS IS FINE] … Thomas Edison had established DC as the standard for electricity distribution and was living large off the patent royalties he was in no mood to lose when George Westinghouse and Nicola Tesla showed up with *alternating current*. Edison's aggressive campaign to discredit the new current took the macabre form of a series of animal electrocutions using AC (a killing process he referred to snidely as getting "Westinghoused"). [source: WIRED, Jan 4, 2000]

A FAILURE TO COMPLY … the line - "Scissored in the Hands of an Angry God!" is a word play on the Jonathon Edwards sermon titled: Sinners in the Hands of an Angry God (July 8. 1741)

… "Après moi, le deluge" – 'After me, the flood' – is generally regarded as a nihilistic expression of indifference to whatever happens after one is gone, attributed to Louis XV.

BLU-82 … Bomb Live Unit-82: has been retired as of July 2008. Used in Viet Nam, it was resurrected during Desert Storm.

… PATHOLOPOLIS: the city of mental, moral, and bodily disorders (Lewis Mumford)

… in this best of all possible worlds – The phrase " *the best of all possible worlds* " was coined by the German polymath and Enlightenment philosopher Gottfried Leibniz, and satirized by Voltaire's Dr. Pangloss in Candide

BOUNDARIES … In Pakistan and Afghanistan, the practice of bacha bazi, a form of sexual slavery and prostitution of male adolescents, has existed for centuries. Outlawed by the Taliban, 'dancing' was resumed in Afghanistan under the US military occupation which turned a blind eye.

COLLATERAL … *"Everything we do is a fiction until it's a fact."*– Jeanette Winterson

… "On average police in the United States shoot and kill more than 1,000 people every year" (https://www.washingtonpost.com/graphics/investigations/police-shootings-database/)

CREMAINS … Raku pottery is often fired up to cone 06 for the final firing, which is around 1852F. Cremation has a normal operating temperature of between 1,000- and 2,000-degrees F.

DREAM INTERPRETATION: wherein a footnote reminds us of Gogol's dreams … Saying the Devil played a trick on him, Nikolai Gogol burned some manuscripts which contained most of the second part of his book 'Dead Souls'.

… the footnote is based on testimony from White House aide Cassidy Hutchinson during public hearings of the US House Select Committee on the JAN 6 attack.

... in 1931, Moscow authorities decided to have Gogol's remains transferred to the Novodevichey Cemetery. His body was discovered lying face down, which gave rise to the conspiracy theory that Gogol had been buried alive.

DREAM INTERPRETATION: in which Samuel L. Jackson ... *fools and motherfuckers rule the world...* source is Levertov: from 'Unresolved', iii... "Fools and criminals/ rule the world." Mr Jackson, a well-known actor, is widely thought to be exceptionally skilled in the use of '*motherfucker*'.

DREAMING of Dos Passos ... *Ernest* [Hemingway] *and I used to read the Bible to each other* - is the opening sentence from a Paris Review dos Passos interview (JAN 14, 2015).

... '*Come, and bring a lot of drunks*' was from an invitation to F. Scott Fitzgerald for an art gallery showing he had.

... *Everyman*, an English morality play of the 15th century, allegorically presents the theme of death and the fate of the human soul—of Everyman's soul — as he tries to justify his time on earth.

DST ... the idea for CONTINUITIES/CASE STUDY/TEACHABLE MOMENT and APPLICATIONS comes from anne carson's play – *norma jeane baker of troy.*

FRAGMENTS ... the idea for this poem came from Arthur Sze's poem, *Sightlines*

... 'There is a bomb in Gilead': appears in The Handmaid's Tale by Margaret Atwood

GHOSTS IN THE MACHINE ... In 1949, the British philosopher Gilbert Ryle coined the phrase "ghost in the machine" to describe a concept he disagreed with: that the mind – the ghost – is separate from the body, or the machine.

... '*And If the Nature of Thought Is Not Everywhere the Same*' ... is from the title of Chapter 8 in "THE GEOGRAPHY OF THOUGHT" by Richard E. Nisbett.

GHOSTS OF JIM HARRISON ... Pripyat (the Ghost City) – an abandoned city in northern Ukraine, home to employees of the Chernobyl nuclear power plant, about a mile away

HEADSPACE ... Black – Black was always about Raptus, Lust, Rimbaud & Verlaine... "Verlaine abandoned his wife and baby to pursue the affair, which may have started before Rimbaud turned 17. They abused opium and alcohol, and Rimbaud was notoriously rude, crude and even violent. As their relationship collapsed, Verlaine shot and wounded his lover, for which he spent 18 months in prison."
[NY Times article, by Antonella Francini - Nov. 1, 2020]

IN SILENT CRISIS WITH OUR PERCEPTIONS ... 'long, long sleep' – Emily Dickinson

LIVIN' THE DREAM ... postcards from Witkiewicz: Stanisław Ignacy Witkiewicz; Polish artist, novelist, metaphysician, narcotics buff [cocaine, mescaline, peyote, nicotine and alcohol], and groundbreaking dramatist, active before World War I and during the interwar period. Although he committed suicide in 1939, rumors emerged that his suicide had been fabricated when a series of postcards in his handwriting began showing up, mailed from 1950 onwards.

MAGA ... President Trump condemned the "Indigenous Peoples Day of Rage" protests in Portland, Ore., calling for law enforcement to arrest the demonstrators; in private meetings, the 'Law and Order President' reportedly was saying things like, "*Just shoot them – crack their skulls.*"

...'We hold these truths to be self-evident', is from the preamble to The Declaration of Independence

... the footnote was sourced from Principles of Good Policing: Avoiding Violence Between Police and Citizens @ www.usdoj.gov/crs. I added the crossed out words.

MIDNIGHT RAIN ... A cardinal number is the number of elements of a set, finite or infinite. In set theory, an infinite set is a set that is not a finite set. Infinite sets may be countable or uncountable. (Wikipedia)

MR DUBITO SEZ ... my wallpaper and I are [not] fighting... is taken from Oscar Wilde's alleged last words

MR DUBITO's Predominant Symptomatology at the Time of Evaluation ... Questions are from a Psychosis Test at Mental Health America - https://www.mhanational.org

ON THE SIXTH DAY ... "Be there, will be wild!": At 1:42 a.m. on Dec. 19, 2020 - shortly after a six-hour Oval Office meeting described by a White House aide as "unhinged" - Donald Trump sent this tweet about a planned protest on January 6, 2021

... "I was slipping in people's blood.": Caroline Edwards, Capitol Police, officer testifying to the JAN 6 Committee

OVID'S CLOWNS ... that which was; that which is; that which may yet be – is based upon Ovid's *Metamorphoses Book XV*: "For that which once existed is no more, and that which was not has come to be; and so the whole round of motion is gone through again."

REDEMPTION ... based on a NY Times article [April 24, 2010] describing the WTU as a warehouse for despair where, "fed a diet of powerful prescription pills and treated harshly by noncommissioned officers," many soldiers said their treatment there made their suffering worse.

SEARCHING FOR THE VOICE THAT IS …"searching for the voice that is great within us" is from the title of the 1970 anthology The Voice That Is Great Within Us: American Poetry of the Twentieth Century, edited by Hayden Carruth. Mr Dubito… is based upon Zbigniew Herbert's 'Mr Cogito'; Dubito is a Latin word meaning 'I doubt'.

TEMPTATION … "Fire and Ice" is a short poem by Robert Frost that discusses the end of the world, likening the elemental force of fire with the emotion of desire, and ice with hate.

THAT, MR DUBITO, is the wrong question … source is the 2004 sci-fi movie "I Robot"

THE KULESHOV EFFECT … The Kuleshov Effect is a film editing technique that changes the meaning of a shot based on the context of a montage, the idea being that individual shots need not have meaning by themselves; their meaning is created by juxtaposition with other shots.

TWENTY QUESTIONS … Keats's plea – he asked to have carved into his gravestone only these words, not his name: "Here lies One Whose Name was writ in Water."

… the tattletale - A white crow, which the Greek God Apollo had left to guard Coronis, informed him of an affair with Ischys, son of Elatus. Apollo, enraged that the bird had not pecked out Ischys's eyes as soon as he approached Coronis, flung a curse upon it so furious that it scorched its feathers, which is why all crows are black. (source: hellenicaworld.com)

WHEN THOSE CURSÉD ENTER FLAMES … from Mozart, Requiem, K. 626: Confutatis;

… A cephalophore is a saint who is generally depicted carrying his or her own severed head.

WOODED MOUNTAINS … 'that story about wheat and weeds' finds its source in a parable – Mathew 13: 24-30

… "the culture of make-believe' is from a Derrick Jensen book title

:: EPILOGUE ::

Monday – 6/23/2025

We Remain - One Nation - Under GUNS

[knives, vehicular assaults, Executive Orders, DOGE, ICE, the National Guard, & Marines]

[Gun Violence: There were 10 *mass* shootings over the weekend: 5 were killed/52 were injured]

Pakistan condemned the Tiny-Fisted Emperor — for bombing Iran: [BOMB BOMB BOMB BOMB BOMB Iran!] — less than 24 hours after saying he deserved a Nobel Peace Prize for defusing a recent crisis with India.   So sad. ☹

"*CONGRATULATIONS TO EVERYONE! It has been fully agreed by and between Israel and Iran that there will be a Complete and Total CEASEFIRE,*" the Trumpinator proclaimed in a social media post Monday. Meanwhile, Iran described the cessation of hostilities as a "*halting of retaliatory strikes*" against Israel.

This year's NATO summit opened Tuesday, attended by a disengaged United States, which seems bent on fighting its own battles, rather than helping European allies with the increased threat from Russia.

In domestic news, the Supreme Court will now allow the MAGA administration to deport immigrants with criminal records to ~~shithole~~ 'third' countries where they have no ties and [bonus!] may face torture.

Florida is building a mass tent temporary detention center [!] - dubbed 'Alligator Alcatraz' [!] - to hold migrants in the Everglades. DHS Secretary Kristi ~~Gnome~~ Noem said the facility's estimated $450M annual operating cost would be funded "*in large part*" by FEMA[!] … which is being dismantled.

U.S. intelligence intercepted Iranian officials privately saying Angry Creamsicle's airstrikes caused less damage than expected. Boy, how time flies. Remember back in 2018, when our uniquely underqualified president withdrew from the Obama-era nuclear deal, which allowed Iran to restart key bomb-making work that he's now trying to ~~obliterate~~ put an end to by, with, and through military ~~force~~ diplomacy?

Meanwhile, back in the good ol' USA, heavily armed, masked commandos continued keeping us safe from "*the worst of the worst illegal alien criminals*" by ~~abducting~~ detaining unsavory landscapers, convictable car wash workers, perverted Wal Mart greeters, treasonable tamale makers, insidious swap meet fans, and loathsome, scheming mothers of children with cancer.

* * *

(Mr Dubito is evaluated by Federal Thought Police)

Mr. Dubito, I want you to pretend you're a tree. Can you do that for me?

Rising, Mr Dubito extends his arms, spreads his fingers, and imaginatively sez
— I have to *leaf* now. May the *forest* be with you —

(inwardly, Mr. Dubito smiles knowing he has nailed a nuanced, multi-layered response)

Umm, right. Can you give me an example of synergy?

Yes! Oh yes!!
That's like when *'assassin-for-hire'* Wade Wilson [Ryan Reynolds]
and Logan [Hugh Jackman] get together and become even *more*
amazing in the love/hate bromance 'Deadpool & Wolverine'!!!

(Mr. Dubito cannot believe his luck. His awareness of here and now is unmatched.)

Mm-hmm ... tell me something interesting about your family.

When vacationing, my parents would often visit a local
cemetery, lie down, and pretend they were buried there.

Yes, that sounds ... never mind. Tell me, what's 'your' favorite childhood memory?

Puberty!!

(Unintelligible) – Well, right, of course, thank you for that.
Last question ... What makes you unique?

Virtue!!

Help me out here. What do you mean by virtue?

In time of drought
a man of virtue
does not pray
for rain

In time of drought
a man of virtue, must still
each day
run toward the sun